RACING IN PLACE

Michael Martone

MICHAEL MARTONE (signature)

RACING IN PLACE

COLLAGES

FRAGMENTS

POSTCARDS

RUINS

The University of Georgia Press   Athens and London

Published by The University of Georgia Press
Athens, Georgia 30602
© 2008 by Michael Martone
All rights reserved

Set in Sabon by Graphic Composition, Inc.
Printed and bound by Thomson-Shore
The paper in this book meets the guidelines for permanence
and durability of the Committee on Production Guidelines
for Book Longevity of the Council on Library Resources.

Printed in the United States of America
12 11 10 09 08 P 5 4 3 2 1

Library of Congress Cataloging-in-Publication Data
Martone, Michael.
Racing in place : collages, fragments, postcards, ruins / Michael Martone.
    p. cm.
ISBN-13: 978-0-8203-3039-6 (pbk. : alk. paper)
ISBN-10: 0-8203-3039-6 (pbk. : alk. paper)
I. Title.
PS3563.A7414Z473 2008
814'.53—dc22   2007019176

British Library Cataloging-in-Publication Data available

These are for

Susan Neville

Il miglior fabbro

CONTENTS

ACKNOWLEDGMENTS

I thank the editors of the books and magazines where these essays first appeared. "Racing in Place" was written for *A Year in Place*, edited by W. Scott Olsen and Bret Lott and published by the University of Utah Press, and was reprinted in *Fourth Genre*. "City Light and Power" first appeared in *Fort Wayne* magazine. "Fore" appeared in *Alabama Literary Journal*, edited by Jay Lamar. "What I Want to Tell" was published by *Michigan Quarterly Review*, edited by Laurence Goldstein. "Going Up" was published by Stephanie G'Schwind in *Colorado Review*. "Still Life of Sidelines with Bob" was published in *Notre Dame Review*, edited by William O'Rourke. "My Father Has Been Turned into a Monstrous Vermin" appeared in the *Seattle Review* as "Mascots" and as "A Menagerie of Mascots" in *In the Middle of the Middle West*, an anthology edited by Becky Bradway. "Ephemera" was commissioned by *Ninth Letter* and Philip Graham. "Sympathetic Pregnancies" appeared in *Scoot Over Skinny*, edited by Donna Jarrell and Ira Sukrungruang. "Seven Dwarf Essays" was commissioned by Kate Bernheimer for her anthology *Brothers & Beasts*, published by Wayne State University Press and reprinted in *Cream City Review*. "Sixteen Postcards from Terra Incognita" appeared in *PRISM international*. "Views of My Glasses" was first published in *Ninth Letter*. "Thirteen Ways of Looking at the Moon Winx" was first published as "An Ode to the Moon Winx Lodge Sign" in *Oxford American*. And "On Being" appeared in a special edition of *Denver Quarterly*, edited by Paul Maliszewski.

Thanks to the quilting bee in Alabama—Sandy Huss, Robin Behn, Wendy Rawlings, Joel Brouwer, Joyelle McSweeney, Patti White, Kate Bernheimer, Philip Beidler, John Crowley, and all of my colleagues in the Indiana limestone-clad Morgan Hall. Praise be to all my students past and present. Paul Maliszewski, Tobin Anderson, Vince Standley, Linda Perla, Deb Unferth, Steve Fellner, Steve Featherstone, Robin Black, Diana Joseph, Sandy Jacobs, Jane Dupuis, Kim Kazemi, Peggy Shinner, Sara Jane Stoner, Jennie VerSteeg, Cynthia Reeves, and Allison Wade. Glory be to the correspondents who received the postcards. Sejal Shah, Brenda Mills, Adria Bernardi, Lea Powers, Pat Warrick, Jean Harper, Rikki Ducornet, Jay Brandon, Ted Bonar, Charlie Baxter, Lex Williford. And thanks be to those who've pieced these pieces together. Mike Wilkerson, Michael Rosen, Nancy Esposito, Monroe Engel, Ann Jones, Kathy Hall, Marilyn Sandidge, Melanie Rae Thon, Valerie Miner, Chris Leland and Osvaldo Sabino, Chris Riley and Mark Feldman, Joe Geha and Fern Kupfer, Steve Pett and Clare Cardinal. Valerie Berry used 3–0 Ethilon black monofilament nylon nonabsorbable surgical suture to tie things up. Marian Young, my secret agent, Stephen Barnett, and the folks at the press patched the book together. Sam and Nick worked the puzzle. And Theresa shored up all the rest.

RACING IN PLACE

In the Middle of Things

AN INTRODUCTION OR AN AFTERWORD

This book is a mess. Well, not this book, the one you are read-ing now, the finished product with its finished pages, its finished cover. A few weeks ago, I responded to the author's question-naire, a marketing survey so extensive and detailed that you lose track of what you once thought you knew about your own book while writing catchy pitches for ad copy and sales meet-ings. I wrote addresses, too, of critics and reviewers who, by now, have or haven't written reviews about the book. Reviewers often don't even receive finished copies of the book, but bound galleys instead, which warn not to quote from this version be-cause things are still uncorrected, unproofed, unfinished, and in flux. And Alison Lerner, in marketing, recently requested cover ideas she'd then forward to design and production and needed a new picture of me, as the one I had sent didn't have the digital oomph she needed for reproduction. My ideas for a cover were a collage of blimp and zeppelin photos or, maybe, a plate of one of the Gee's Bend quilts, long on tour but now making their way back home to Alabama. I don't know, now as I write this, what the cover actually is, nor any of the versions or mock-ups. You, the reader of this introduction, do know (in this other now, the now of your reading the finished book). And I don't know who

1

they finally got to blurb the book, though I just sent a note of some names of people who might want to read these essays in typescript and e-mail a few sentences back to Athens. The flap copy needs to be written, telegraphic paragraphs the book reps can use to pitch to bookstore buyers sometime in the future. I haven't done it yet, but I will probably go up to Chicago in the fall to the Great Lakes Booksellers Association meeting and hang around the table manned by the Miller Brothers, the regional distributors for the press, promoting the finished product to the dwindling number of bookstore owners and managers in the hope that they will order a copy or two of the book that, right now as I write this, is in parts and pieces, unfinished and even unbegun, on disks and scrap paper in Athens, Tuscaloosa, and Fort Wayne. That all has yet to be done along with this introduction that is only as far along as this word I am typing right now. So the now of this book, the book that is (as I write this right now) a mess, is not the book of the now *now*, the moment now that you are reading this *this*.

But that's the way it always is. The process of book production is obscured, mystified, it seems, a lot by the complex nature of the actual making, but a little bit intentionally (on the part of authors, agents, and publishers) to give the work a sheen of magic, a gloss of spontaneity. You, reader, who admire books, share with the devotees of legislation and sausages the admonition that one shouldn't track the way laws, links, or books are being made. A book, especially, wants to appear parthenogenetic. And that's particularly funny as the publisher of this book is headquartered in a town named after the goddess who, as Zeus's afterthought, embodied forethought, fully armored and ready to rumble, sprang from some mythic migraine. We'd like to think a writer writes something someplace and the pages are sent off and after awhile a book springs forth, hot type and all, and appears on a shelf someplace. But buried there in the process is my early query letter to Nicole Mitchell, the press's director, and the negotiations with Andrew Berzanskis, the acquiring editor, who rounded up the anonymous readers—anonymous to me still—who wrote reports for the press's Board of Directors, who signed off on what was then a pile of loose paper with notations from Andrew that the title probably will be changed and the two brief essays will be scrapped and, oh yes, the introduction is to come, the author, in Alabama, having some difficulty writing it, not even sure the book needs an introduction and unsure what the introduction should say at this point. And the holidays are approaching, so that means that Andrew won't even have a contract until the first of the year and it, the contract, unwritten, will have to be vetted by my agent, Marian Young, who will attach her clause with her mailing address in New York, instructing that any money that the book produces will be sent first to her before it comes back to me, and she will make a good case that I receive more complimentary copies of the finished book when it is finished than the paltry number the boilerplate specifies. And I won't even go into the copyediting because I don't know at this point who will be editing this, though I hope it is Mindy Wilson, a freelance editor I worked with the last time and who was, ten years ago, my student at the University of Alabama. I directed her writing of her thesis, a book of stories, the first thesis I directed at Alabama. I went through the book peppering Mindy with questions as she now is (or soon will be) going through this book, tabbing her questions with bright-colored Post-it notes. But that is all in the future, though now, now that you are reading this, it is in the past.

So the book is a mess. And it is a book of smaller messes. I even subtitled the book "Collages, Fragments, Postcards, Ruins," or at least it was subtitled this when I submitted the book. In the editing process since then, the subtitle might have been left out. That is to say the essays collected here were written at different times for different occasions and in forms that are episodic at best, anecdotal, associative, nonsequential, inconsequential, random. They don't shape up into much of a narrative pattern, I can see, with attention to beginnings, middles, and ends. To me, it seems like a lot of middles. That has always seemed like the problem for the memoir (and you can think of this book as a collection of little memoirs). How does one make sense of what's going on when it is still going on? Writing about life should be the providence of the eulogist, who gets the high ground of a coda, a cessation of event and the relative stability of the facts to inject some meaning, some sense, into the stuff that has been happening and now has happened. Memoirs are artificial eulogies often with the memoirist looking to draw parentheses around a portion of a messy, spontaneous, ongoing life (childhood, say, or that eventful summer or the year spent abroad). It's over, a curious phrase. Memoirists have to find an "over." It is funny then that this essay, the one I am writing now, is an introduction to a book of memoirs, but it is the last thing written. Maybe it should come as an afterword. Who knows? Maybe this is there at the end of the finished book already. But if this is at the end of the book you are reading, it is after the other essays and will be agreeing (or not) with the assessment of what this book means. If this introduction stays in the front of the book, that means that, even though it was written in hindsight, it is working (or not) as a kind of foreshadowing. Either way, it is trying to make a sense of what's going on, a parenthesis, as I said, attempting to bring some stability to the whole shifting mix of things, events, notions, stray thoughts, and odd facts. Maybe this introduction should be both published as a before and after. Though the words remain the same, the essay would change, be read differently on the occasion of the reading and on what comes after and before its reading and its rereading. Never stepping into the same river twice and all that.

To tell you the truth, the difficulty of writing this introduction didn't delay it, Andrew. Nor did my ambivalent feelings about "introductions" being generated for these kinds of books. Truth is, life and time got in the way. I am in Fort Wayne again, where I was born and grew up, a place that I have written about and will continue to write about, I suppose, even though I haven't lived here in a quarter century, half my life. For a while I thought this introduction would make clear that the essays collected here, written over the last ten years, marked some kind of transition away from writing about Fort Wayne, about the Midwest. These essays were all written in the time I've lived in Alabama, and maybe there is something to be said of that. But right now, I am back up North tending my mother, who is in the hospital, uterine cancer, and in the long hours in waiting rooms and at my patient mother's bedside waiting, I have been piecing together this, this something. I guess now it is the introduction to the book, the book whose many parts are beginning to come together as a book down South in my other home.

My mother's surgery took place at Parkview Hospital a few days ago. Parkview was once on the edge of town, it even overlooked parkland that now is crowded with clinics and offices and assisted living facilities and parking structures. The hospital itself, at its inception a modest modernist box, has expanded, morphing with all the subsequent additions of the last half-century of medical science. There are wards for cancer, cardiac, and rehab, and the hotel-like annex for birthing that in the past was known as delivery. There is a hospice. Right outside my mother's window on the surgical recovery floor is the seemingly precariously perched landing pad on stilts flooded by light at night. The two evac helicopters are constantly taking off and landing, hovering nosily a few dozen yards away as the pilots change the pitch on the rotors to land or veer away. As my mother sleeps, I write postcards. I tell my correspondents that this hospital is the site of my earliest memory. My younger brother, Tim, was born here, and back then floors were quarantined to siblings, I guess, so I remember being in a little parking lot way below, hoisted on my father's shoulders, looking up to the fifth floor and a big plate-glass window where my mother waved down to me. A couple years later when I was five I almost died here in the very same hospital, a tonsillectomy that had its complications, my mother then at my bedside hysterical as I hemorrhaged, outdoing Shirley MacLaine in *Terms of Endearment* screaming for help at the nurses' station. Or so she tells me in her lucid moments between the pain and zonked-out state after she presses the button of the morphine pump. It isn't morphine, and I will have to find out the actual name of the drug. But my mother is having some trouble getting the knack of its delivery sequence, and there are signs that warn that only the patient can push the button, so all I can do is coach.

The doctors and nurses get the patients up and walking right away. The pressure of insurance oversight drives this, of course, but it reflects also the newer theories of healing to slough the heavy anesthesia, wake the body up, ward off ilea. So now I am walking with my mother, feeble, a few hours after surgery, down the corridor. First to the nurses' station, then a few hours later down to the conference room and back. The elevator lobby, the waiting lounge, then the next time the second nurses' station in the west wing, a little farther each time. We are aiming for the far end of the hallway and the big plate-glass picture-window wall shimmering there like a mirage. It looks out to the west at a sunset you can see framed there even at this distance.

Before my mother's surgery, she performed a novena at St. Jude's church and dedicated the prayers to St. Anthony. She hedged her bet, the two patron saints of lost causes, of miracles. We will be able to see the church where she prayed from that window, too, and Mom thinks that will be a good ending to that beginning, further motivation propelling these painful walks. And I think now that the window off in the distance might be the very same window I remember my mother, framed there almost fifty years ago, waving and waving down at me. Maybe it was the floor below or the one above but it was this side of the hospital, the end of another long walk. I imagine that when we get there, lugging the wheeled metal Christmas tree decked with the beeping IV pumps and tubes, the bags of saline, glucose, and dope, I'll mention this to my mother, this strange shift in time and place and point of view, how this shuffling dance we are doing couldn't have been scripted any better. The sunset, the saints, the son. How it all makes sense somehow. But that walk hasn't happened yet, or it hasn't happened yet right now, the moment I am writing this. Perhaps, as you read this, it has. Mom has had the staples removed, is resting comfortably at home, the cancer banished for the present. Christmas has come and New Year's, too. I have written this introduction and the press in Athens has chosen to keep it in the book. But right now (right now) both helicopters, both on some urgent missions of rescue or recovery, are floating in the air outside this hospital room window. One is taking off, one about to land, I am not sure which is which as they both slowly circle, carefully maneuvering through this specific time, this particular place, this exact concoction of memory.

Racing in Place

33 HOOSIER HAIKU

1

The first thing you did was tune in the radios. Everyone had the new transistor radios, most the size of cigarette packs, in pastel hard-shell plastic. Some were upholstered with protective leatherlike vinyl with flaps and snaps and die-cut openings for the gold-embossed tuning dials, a slit for the coin-edged volume wheel, an aperture for the ear jack, out of which an always too-short and easily kinked wire attached to a single waxy plug you screwed into your head. But today, race day, no one listens to the 500 on the earphone. My father and the other fathers in the neighborhood are pouring a patio. It's what they do on Memorial Day.

2

The elms, for some reason, haven't died on Parnell Avenue, and their vaulting branches arch over the street, throwing it into deep shade. The parade route runs from State Boulevard along Parnell out to the War Memorial Coliseum. We like to sit near the Dairy Queen, unfolding our lawn chairs in the parking lot driveway. We have brought the big radio with the stitched handle. It is the size of my school lunch box. The cars at the track make a swishing sound as they zoom about. I sit on the curb and think I see the horses' hooves throwing sparks. A semi-trailer is hauling a retired F-86 from the airbase out to be displayed on the Coliseum's lawn. The Navy Club's bus-long gray destroyer, number 48, floats by above me, its wheels hidden by a skirt of waves.

3

My mother and the other mothers are sitting on the patio next door, a concrete slab in the middle of the yard. It is cured to a marble white. The furniture is new, webbed candy-colored nylon and aluminum tubing. The Thompsons' patio. It was poured last year. The men are wearing white T-shirts, khaki pants, and their old work shoes, standing in a circle around the wheelbarrow filled with crushed ice and bottles of Old Crown beer, tuning in, each one holding his little radio next to his ear, worrying the tuning dial, thumbing up the volume. One by one they find WOWO, the local station on the network, coax the static into sound, cocking the radios at angles to align their tiny antennae. It is primitive. It is magic. It is like they are blowing on smoldering tinder to get it to spark. And they do.

4

The thrum of the engines brought us outside. We looked up shading our eyes against the sun. The blimp was just above the tops of the dying elm trees and descending it seemed toward the field behind our house. Then there was a change in the engines' pitch and the blimp yawed and floated up and away. We ran to the car to follow, slowly cruising through the meandering neighborhood streets. Stretched out on the back seat of the '57 Chevy, I looked up at the blimp as it wallowed overhead, framed first in the back window then in the one at my feet then in the one above my head as it maneuvered and my father, turning, came about and circled beneath it. It settled, at last, in a field near the three rivers, a ground crew hauling it down. The cars that had been chasing it parked in a big ring around it. It was May, and the blimp was on its way to take up station above

Indianapolis. Moored, it levitated a few feet off the ground. We all sat transfixed on the car's hood and watched the blimp float but stay perfectly still.

5

Another radio joins the nest of transistor radios on the grass nearby, amplifying the tinny voice of Sid Collins, the Voice of the Indianapolis 500. The men begin to work, finishing the frame and leveling the bed while others mix the cement and sand. I hear beneath the Voice in the grass a sound like static but it isn't static. It is the pulsing siren of the racers' engines flying around the track, the two-beat peal as they scream past the mic, an "ee" then a long "em." *EEmmmmm*. But so small, an insect humming in the greening grass. There will be locusts this summer idling in the trees. Summer is racing toward us. I coast my bike down the Kaimeiers' drive, join the other kids on their bikes doing laps around the manhole covers on either end of the street.

6

I go to college in Indianapolis. My mother went to the same school. Near noon, I cross the muddy campus. I slog along on the way to class. The bells ring out, as they do every hour, every day, the opening bars of "Back Home Again in Indiana." It is a gray day with the clouds lowering. It is often gray, the result of the atmospheric accident in which we live. Ground zero for an occluded ceiling generated by the lakes, the wind, the flat flat ground. Back home again in Indiana, I whisper, where the sun refuses to shine. Then in the silence after the tolling, I hear a distant screech, a prehistoric trumpet, a beast's yawning scream originating high up in cavities of a skull. The scraps of sound drift in the thick air. Tire tests at the track across town.

7

The race is on on the kitchen radio. I sit at the kitchen table coloring in the outlines of racecars. My mother has drawn a simple template—a side view of two wheels, the tube of the fuselage, a wedge of windshield, a hump of the rear engine. I have traced out thirty-three copies, placing a clean sheet of paper on top of her drawing and following the outline. Now I am coloring each a different color. On the radio there are announcers in each turn of the track and on the straightaways. They follow the leader around the lap. Sid Collins, the Voice of the Indianapolis 500, says that this is the greatest spectacle in racing. But I've never seen it. It is only on the radio. The table is layered with the brightly colored cars, scrambled together, a wreck of color. I stay inside the lines I've outlined in black. I know that the shades of green are unlucky. The blues are beautiful and limitless. Outside my father is mowing the lawn. I hear the mower's engine fade as he goes around the far side of the house.

8

There are high-school bands but they are mostly quiet, saving their practiced marches for the reviewing stands on the other side of the river. The drummers thump a cadence of the wood sticks against the metal rims of their drums. They slide their feet on each step. I see green puttees and canvas gaiters of the Legion and the VFW posts' colors. It is strangely quiet for a parade. The swish of cloth. The silky flags sliding along the polished poles. The whispered humph, humph of a drill sergeant. Each unit slowly disappears down the dappled tunnel of the street. The drive shaft turns beneath the flatbed truck, an honor guard, at parade rest around a mock-up of a tomb on the carpeted bed. In the silence, the echoes of hundreds of portable radios. The race in Indianapolis, a hollow drone.

9

My father drilled a hole in a rubber-coated baseball, threaded a rope through it and knotted the end so it wouldn't slip back through. On the other end of the rope was a handle. In the field behind the house, he twirled the ball around above his head. I stood to one side with a bat and tried to hit it as he banked it toward me. It zoomed by. I was getting my timing back for summer, he said. A garbage can lid was on the ground, a makeshift home plate. The ball wobbled, warbled a hiss as it made its orbit. Around and around. I'd catch it coming in the corner of my eye and step into the approaching sound.

10

The simulators were painted gunmetal and arranged three to the row before the movie screen. I was driving through a neighborhood like mine though its colors were faded or too brightly lit. There were people walking on the sidewalks wearing clothes from when I was a kid. The women wore white gloves and hats with net veils; the men wore suits and ties. A freckled boy, his head shaved, broke away from his parents and darted out into the street lined with old elms. I seemed to slow to a stop. The machine in the back whirred and clicked, recording whether or not my brake pedal was depressed. Then I was entering a highway, a new interstate, its concrete brilliant white. All the turn indicators were ticking in the room. Then it was raining and it was night. I'd glance at the speedometer from time to time as I was instructed. The needle slowly swept around from zero as I sped up. The room filled with a throaty engine noise. The sound track ran through the gearbox. The brakes complained slightly as I pulled into the driveway of a house like my house. The machine in the back came on again to see if I had put the car in park and turned the key to stop the engine. I had put the car in park. I had turned the key. I waited a few more minutes, my seat belt buckled, until the bell rang for the next class.

11

I remember the smell of the newspaper, the way it was folded to the page with the starting grid, the ten rows of three cars each, the blocks of information—number, driver, owner, sponsor, engine, body, speed. My father's scribbled notes as each car dropped out of the race. Engine. Transmission. Tires. Crash. My mother finishing up the dishes picked up the coffee cup my father had forgotten he used to weigh the edges of the paper down. There was a blot staining the top of the statistics, a blurred circle, smeared, smearing. My father sat and listened to the race's murmur, my baseball mitt on one hand, the other hand rubbing the neat's-foot oil into the darkening pocket.

12

The pace car moved by at the walking pace of the parade. We were on the Parnell bridge over the St. Joe. Ricky Brown was going on about the 'Vette, the particulars of its engine displacement, the block's bore, the compression ratio. A girl from our high school was a queen of something that year, and she waved at us. Too cool, all of us but Ricky turned away from the parade and, leaning on the bridge's railing, looked at the river just below the deck, swollen and running fast in spring. Ricky called out to the guy driving the car, hunched over listening to the radio, "Who's leading? What lap?"

13

A Saturday before the race, I went with my dad to May Sand and Stone to pick up the bags of cement and sand. He had an Olds Cutlass coup, white with a blue top and bucket seats. In high school I would total it, running off the road into the ditch. The windows were cranked down and the radio was cranked up high to the time trials. We followed the trace out to the gravel pit. I liked hearing about the driver on the bubble, the slowest car about to be bumped by another qualifier. The overgrown ditch on the side of the road was all that was left of the canal built to connect the Great Lakes with the Mississippi, bankrupting Indiana before the Civil War. The water was stagnant and weedy. On the bobbing cattails, red wing blackbirds perched. Their calls were like the rattles of mixing balls in cans of spray paint.

14

Small planes circled, dots followed by a dash of their banners, their advertisements, unreadable from this distance, tracing their spiraling paths. I was driving home, north, to Fort Wayne. I took the wrong exit on purpose to circle the city the long way around so I could listen to the race. The radio said the race was halfway through and under a yellow caution flag. A survivor of the most recent wreck was thanking God. Thirty-three miles of four-lane beltway until I-69. I worked my way between the other cars and trucks, racing. I could not see the track from the highway, just the planes trailing their exhaust of messages, circling above it in the distance.

15

The race, on the radio, is background, drowned out by the stutter of the electric clippers my father uses to sculpt the hedge in the backyard. His shirt is off, stuffed into his back pocket. It looks like a tail. Mother sits on the chaise lounge on our slab of a patio, painting her toenails a bright red. Two orange extension cords snake out through the grass, one winding toward the radio and one attaching to the clippers. We've planted impatiens in the shade of the garage, the egg carton nursery flats nest inside each other. I coil the hose next to the spigot. Maybe later we will wash the car.

16

I walked to my high school. I took State Boulevard, which was an old township road running east and west that had, when the city grew up around it, become a main cross-town corridor. When I walked it, during the rush hours, I kept pace with the cars crawling along in the daily traffic jams. Sometimes a string of cars would break away only to stall again at the next light, a half block ahead, where I would catch up again. Ahead of me was my high school, North Side, across the St. Joseph River from the Old Crown Brewery. It was spring. The brewery made the neighborhood reek of fermented spent grain. Behind me was North Highlands, where I lived and where, as it was high ground, the radio and television stations planted their transmission towers. Coming home, I saw the strobing beacons on each become visible as the sun set and the city grew dark. The cars creeping along next to me in the street had their windows down. It was spring. The patter of the radio leaked out. A song, a weather report, the ninth caller. As I walked along, the volume seemed to fade and pulse with the strips of tiny suspended warning lights at the other end of the road.

17

A sign says this is the deepest hole in Indiana. Empty yellow dump trucks follow the access road cut into ledges screwing down to the quarry's floor where groaning excavators gnaw at a trench. I am in a metal observation cage extending out over the lip of the pit looking down forever. The loaded trucks spiral up, trudging around ever-widening loops scored against the sloping walls to the top. The reports from the track of the time trials and practice laps are running on the PA system interrupted by an announcement that someone's order has been filled or someone else has a phone call. Dust steams up to the brim. I am floating above the dust swirling below me, looking at it roil through the open steel grid at my feet. Suddenly, Phantoms from Baer Field rip by overhead, practicing the Memorial Day fly-by.

18

"Stay tuned to the greatest spectacle in racing," the voice on the radios said. The transistor radios seemed to be fading, their batteries taxed. The cement of the patio was setting up. In a corner of the slab, our fathers allowed us to write our names with a ten-penny nail and press our handprints into the spongy surface. We washed our hands at the spigot, a puddle of mud forming at our feet. We stretched out on the grass. A tire commercial. A milk commercial. An interview in the pits. The cars roaring by drowned out the people speaking. I tried to hold the level level. I held it above me, up to the sky, nudging the bubble back and forth between the hairlines in its little yellow tube of fluid.

19

My mother went to the race once. When she was in college in Indianapolis, women from her sorority rode in the festival parade before the start in vintage cars around the track. My mother rode in a horseless carriage made by Studebaker. She wore an antique duster and a big hat with goggles. She waved to all the people in the grandstands, a half a million people. The speedway becomes the second largest city in Indiana on the day of the race, she always says. Making deviled eggs on Memorial Day, flicking the dollop of yolk mixed with mayonnaise in the cup of the hollowed half, dusting the two dozen halves with paprika and pepper, she remembers the boxed lunch she ate that day in the sunny stands, the race itself an intermittent distraction in the background.

20

When I was in kindergarten, I was in the parade. I rode a float, sitting in a lawn glider that glided back and forth beneath an arching garden arbor decorated with paper roses and on a lawn of artificial grass staked with lawn flamingoes and a plastic bird-bath with real water that got us wet when the wind blew. A white Impala pulled the trailer, and my father was in the back seat looking out the back window up at me riding on the glider. I wore a crown I kept for years afterward on the globe in my room. I remember the old trees making a roof over us, how slow we went down Parnell, the way people on each side of the street waved with one hand while the other hand held a radio to an ear.

21

The high school loop ran north and south from one Azar's Big Boy to the other through the center of town. The lights were timed and we hit every one, not stopping. We went over rivers and under overpasses where sometimes hulking Nickel Plate or Wabash trains clanked on tracks above us. The streets were the old state highways, wide and one way, lined with glass-globed lights still painted on the top to black them out from the air. You couldn't be too careful. We talked, my buddies and me, about going to Ohio, where they sold 3.2 beer to minors, but we never did. We were unable to escape the gravitational pull of the place. Our high school going by. The musk of the brewery and the slow-moving river choked with cottonwood. WOWO on the radio. "I have no desire to ever see that race. You sit in one place and see the cars for, what?, a second or so and then wait a couple of minutes for it to happen again." There, the neon cross of Calvary Temple. There, the old City Light power house. There, the armory. Powers Hamburgers. The Lincoln Tower. The Old Fort, a replica of the old fort, a guard walking the walls looking out for the vandals we fancied ourselves to be.

22

I have a picture of my mother and father sitting on their graves. Always planning ahead, they purchased the plots in the Catholic cemetery years ago. They bought the monuments too, already engraved with their names and birthdates. They were optimistic enough not to have the 19 of the death date inscribed, but their names are there and their birthdates. The markers are simple slabs of polished granite the size and shape of swing set seats, very low to the ground. It looks as if they are sitting on the ground. They are smiling. We went there one Memorial Day to look at all the graves. My father's parents' and sister's, my mother's parents' and grandparents'. We ended up checking out how their own graves were doing. There they were. The stones were supposed to be that small and low to make the maintenance of the cemetery efficient. No flowers allowed. There were flags on Memorial Day but those were taken back up after a day or two. In the future, the mowers would cut right over the stones as they sank the rest of the way into the ground.

23

Our bicycles are piled in a wreck we have simulated. We are sprawled, casualties, on the strip of grass between the curb and sidewalk. After a while, we forget we have died. We look up at the streamlined and spoiled clouds, racing.

24

My father went to the time trials one year but it rained. The showers were scattered, and when the sun came out they tried to dry the track by driving ordinary cars and trucks around it.

He sat in the fourth turn and watched fire engines, ambulances, wreckers, buses, and pace cars speed by, accelerating the evaporation. Just as it was drying off, racecars with their big slick tires revving their engines in the pit lane, it rained again. Bored, ushers with opened black umbrellas walked around the two-and-a-half mile oval, and in the homestretch a few of them broke away from the group with longer and longer strides trying to be the first to cross the finish line.

25

Behind the chain link fence, the patients of the State Hospital and Training Center watch the parade. Some of them march along behind the fence, falling into step with the passing bands and color guards or drifting along with the creeping floats. The fence runs for what would be five blocks along Parnell. The streets that dead-end at the boundary of the hospital grounds are used as staging areas for the parade's start. The patients wear hospital gowns and robes of pastel pinks, blues, greens, and yellows. They press their faces into the fence. Some climb a foot or two to get a better view, their fingers wrapped in the weave of the metal links, until the orderlies, who have been listening to the race huddled around the radio in an old ambulance, peel them off and plop them on the ground again. The ones who have been shadowing the parade are stopped when the fence turns a corner blocks away. They race back to the beginning, focus on a new drum major who trills his whistle, high stepping in place. The patients turn with him and begin to march once again.

26

Stuck in the stalled traffic on State, this year's pace car, a red Ford Mustang. The local dealerships of the winning manufacturer would get a shipment of special-edition models each year to show off. You would see them racing around town, advertising the brand's fortune. On each door was a decal of a wheel with wings and the array of all the racing flags. One day each year, pace cars appeared, migratory birds or butterflies. A woman sat at the wheel blowing bubbles of bubble gum. Spring.

27

One year, something happened. A wreck at the start of the race had killed several drivers. I remember listening to the restart in school a day later. I was in art class rolling out clay to coil into pots. Others were kneading the clay or cutting blocks of it with wire. The teacher was firing pieces in the small kiln, and you could hear the whoosh of air as it burned. The announcers at the track were subdued and sad. It seemed the completion of the race was more of a chore now, something that had to be done. The engines sounded muffled. I liked my art class. It was quiet as we worked. The teacher moved from table to table, here smoothing the lip of a pitcher with his thumb, there applying a slip with an old brush. The radio muttered in the corner.

28

Sid Collins, the Voice of the Indianapolis 500, will kill himself. I'll hear the news on a radio in a car in Indiana.

29

We sit on the car hood at the end of the runway. The Phantoms, in formations of two, glide over us, their flaps flared and gear down. In the distance, we see them touch down. Then the afterburners ignite and they leap back up off the shimmering runway. The pilots are logging hours on the weekend. Above us, pairs of jets bank and turn, circling on approach. Climbing, their engines make a sound like ripping blue cloth. Some cars in the race this year have turbine engines. They whine and whistle on the radio, breaking records during practice laps. There's a war. There's always a war. But it is far away.

30

I practice driving in the cemetery. My father sits in the passenger seat playing with the radio. The yellow Rambler is a company car he bought at auction, a decal of the company's logo peeled from the door. It's a big cemetery. In the older part there are old trees and the monuments are columns and urns and obelisks. Wrought iron fences or low walls of stone outline family plots.

The roads curve around in circles. I stop and start and signal. I ease out the clutch, and the engine bucks. I can gain a little speed on the straightaways of the new section where the markers are in ordered rows and next to the ground. Mary, the Mother of God, directs traffic at an intersection. I go by my grandmother's grave again. A troop of Boy Scouts carrying backpacks filled with toy flags sifts between the stones, dipping down to the ground, in ones and twos, to decorate them for the weekend.

31

I walk the sidewalks of the old neighborhood. Summer started after Memorial Day, and I spent those summers riding my bike behind the city crews cutting down the dying trees. The chipper with its long-necked Victrola hood sounded, as it bit into branches, like the whooping engines at Indy howling out of the corners. The people who live here now are not home. At the parade perhaps. Picnicking. At the cemeteries. In cars. At the race. Or on their way someplace listening to the race on the radio. The patio is still here. The owner's just hosed it down, and it is drying in the light breeze and warming sun. My name and the names of my friends. And, there, the dimple of my handprint holding a puddle of water in the depression of the palm. In some other backyard I hear the chirp of a radio.

32

We dream about the moonlight on the Wabash. We sang it before our own bike races along the meandering side streets and oxbow loops of the neighborhood. We sang the song like we heard Jim Nabors sing it on the radio before the race. We tried to swallow the words as we sang them, holding notes on the verge of a yawn. We sounded, to our own ears, operatic and old-fashioned and grown-up. We marveled at the transformation of his voice every time he sang. Our own voices were changing. Things could change. The crowd cheering at the end of the song had one voice, a static static. We could stay out until the streetlights came on. The streetlights came on. We raced our shadows between pools of light. The gibbous globes, dabbed with black paint during the war, were caught glowing softly in the black branches of the leafing trees.

33

I took a job five hundred miles from home. Five hundred miles was what the odometer ticked off as I drove the Dodge Dart from Fort Wayne out to Iowa on old US 30. It took twelve hours with pit stops, the time it would take to run three or four races around the track in Indianapolis. As I drove, I imagined unspooling the concrete of the Speedway, shaking out the kinks of its turns and stretching it straight out behind me. I lost WOWO somewhere near the finish, swallowed in the local chatter of interfering frequencies. At night, though, I heard the edges of it when I was at the edge of sleep. I imagined a pulsating bleat of energy springing from its tower near my old home, the expanding circle of the signal opening from ground zero and rolling toward me. On the edge of sleep, just below hearing, the engine of my own body, the rush of blood in my ear, circulating.

City Light and Power

VIEWS OF MY GRANDFATHER WALKING

In 1930, my grandfather was working on the railroad, the Pennsylvania Railroad to be exact, or "the Pennsy" as he and the rest of Fort Wayne called the PRR. He was then a management trainee, learning the workings of the company by working various jobs in each of the company's divisions. That day in 1930 he was a trackwalker, walking track, gandy dancing minor repairs. His supervisor sidled up to him as he inspected a frog at a junction on the west side. "Jim," the man said to my grandfather, "times are tough. We have to lay you off for a few months." The railroad called him back in 1941. Way before then, my grandfather had found a job working as an orderly at the Irene Byron Sanitarium north of town where he would wheel the TB patients onto the screened-in porches even in the middle of the winter. He'd sometimes take the interurban to and from the hospital grounds, where he would spend the week in a dorm, returning home to the house on Oakland Street to stay a day with his wife and daughter, my mother, who called him Jim and had to be reminded this stranger was her father. Often he'd walk back and forth to save the fare, following the interurban roadbed, inspecting those tracks for free. He was happy when he had the chance to work closer to home and took a job working in the city for the city. When the railroad called him back in 1941, my grandfather had five years under his tool belt reading meters for City Light. He saw no reason to go back, a decade later, to resume his training for the trains.

I hardly remember it now after all these years. It was there at the end of Calhoun Street, arching over the road between the Allen County Jail and the box factory—the City Light sign. A lacy grid of steel girders supported the neon tubing. It looked in my memory like a precarious mesh of rusted struts and guy wires you could easily see through. Could you see too, in the distance, the blocky powerhouse on North Clinton across the river near Lawton Park? You could surely see the smoke billowing from its stacks, the superstructure of the sign back downtown a kind of frame, a parable of power. At night the arching cantilevered metal disappeared in the dark. There floating above the street was the City Light logo, an asymmetric illuminated crossword, the vertical C-I-T-Y intersecting the horizontal L-I-G-H-T, pivoting on the single *i* both words shared. And emanating from that crisscrossed core, zigzagging bolts of lightning bisected the right angles of the words. I remember them flashing, those bolts, but I can't be sure. I can't forget the illusion of those letters floating above Fort Wayne, stitched and twitching against the velvet of the night sky, or its simple message of a C-I-T-Y of light, of L-I-G-H-T all lit up.

My grandfather walked to work to work a job that required walking. He read meters. He walked each day from his house in North Highlands near Hamilton Park a few blocks over from Oakland Street where the family had moved, always stopping on his way downtown at Precious Blood to say a quick prayer in the rear pews of the church, light an old-fashioned candle in the narthex, then walk the rest of the way to the office on Lafayette Street south of the Wabash tracks. I told him once about a story I read called "The End of the Mechanical Age" by Donald Barthelme in which God appears as a character. And how is God depicted? As a meter reader sporting coveralls (like my grandfather) with His flashlight poking out of the back pocket (like my grandfather's). In the story, God was reading the quantity of grace in the world as he went door-to-door. There is something intimate and omniscient to the job my grandfather performed. Because he walked everywhere, the size of the city retreated back down to a human dimension, a human scale, as he transversed it. There is only so much distance one can cover on foot, and that covered distance goes by at a speed that allows one to see and to connect and to remember. He connected, following the power grid of wires that knit the city up. He remembered every kink in the concrete grid of city streets and every square of sidewalk. Each day he took another route out into the city that led him down all the alleys and through the backyards and, in most cases then, underground into people's basements where the meters were kept near the coal bins, the root cellars, and the ash pits. There were people home to let him in the house. "Meter man" was his only password. It was a secular and sacred pilgrimage for him, this daily constitutional. Every day, he walked. He walked in his own footsteps for forty years.

The electricity my grandfather read was the alternating current kind. The electrons stuttered back and forth along the wires' cycle. My grandfather too on his journeys completed daily, weekly, monthlong orbits around the city. He circulated, and because there were periods of time between particular visits, he would notice the changing landscape about him. Citizens tinkered with remodeling, adding a porch or patio, or they let their places go. And all these changes were overlaid with the particulars of the changing seasons. He set meters and shut them off. During the Depression he'd turn off the power at a delinquent house in sight of its unemployed occupants, who supervised his work in silence. A few months later he would be back at the same address to switch the juice back on, the bill now paid. But on the way in he'd pass the gasman there to turn off the gas. The customers had only so much money for the utilities and had run up the one as they paid the other back down. My grandfather witnessed as he walked. Here, this obsolescence, and there, this rebirth.

I have on my key ring a meter seal my grandfather gave me. It's a tab of red plastic, an inch long rounded on one end like the top of a tombstone. The plastic is branded with the initials "CL&P"—City Light and Power. On the other end are slots where two ends of a wire, curled into a loop, can be inserted. After setting a meter, my grandfather would close the access panel and seal it with the device, threading the wire through the grommets on the meter case, then snapping it into the locking plastic tap. If anyone tampered with the meter they would have to break the wire to open the meter case. The meter on my house here in Alabama has the same kind of seal. It is outside, the back of the house. In the summer, you should see the disk inside the meter's glass twirl. The hands on the five dials spin around, recording the usage consumed by the power-hungry air-conditioner. Occasionally I will catch a glimpse of my meter reader as he walks down the side street and slips down the little hill to read my meter. He is there and then he is gone. It seems so old-fashioned still. The meter itself has not changed much from the time of Edison, who probably invented the way to charge for the electricity at the same time he was making the products that used it. And the reader walking, that is just as old-fashioned. You would think they would come up with some other way to check. I suppose they have. The information transmitted electronically or the scoring determined through elaborated mathematical algorithms run by a very distant and stationary computer. Some days, when it isn't too hot, I walk the several miles to work. Chances are I am the only one walking to get someplace. At the office, my coworkers find it curious. The meter seal I mentioned is on my key ring that holds my car key, after all. With each step I take, I hear the tiny tinny clinking in my pocket.

We waited in the dark. A fuse had blown—the electric steam iron tipping the scale. We had fuses, not the more modern circuit breakers, in our house on Clover Lane. My father could easily replace the blown fuse. He worked for the phone company, and had been, like my grandfather, a member of the International Brotherhood of Electrical Workers—the IBEW. I have my grandfather's union buttons. They depict the brotherhood's logo—a hand made into a fist squeezing a bundle of bolting electricity. My father could have switched out the blown fuse but instead called my grandfather, who lived down the hill a dozen blocks away. Getting the call, he strapped on his tool belt. I have the tool belt too. It is a modest one with a single leather pouch equipped with a screwdriver, flashlight, needle-nose pliers, black electrician's tape, wire stripper, and wire cutter. My grandfather headed out, walked down Poinsette along the rim of Hamilton Park and up the hill on Emerson, hardly a walk at all for him. Years later, I realize why we sat in the dark waiting for my grandfather to come fix the fuse. I figure it is kind of a union thing, things electric being the purview of my grandfather, a kind of featherbedding. Even then it was a funny family eccentricity. My family took on the silly inconvenience in order to tease my grandfather's seriousness of purpose and task. But finally this was what my grandfather did his whole life: He went door-to-door bringing light, bringing power. His family could suffer a few minutes of darkness to appreciate that, passing the time by laughing at the picture of that old man wading through the pools of light cast by the street lamps, in his City Light overalls and his worn utility belt riding his hip like a gunslinger, a brand new fuse gripped fast in his fist, striding purposely to our rescue.

Fore

1

My house at 29 Country Club Hills overlooks the old Country Club of Tuscaloosa. The ninth tee and green, a short par 3 of 183 yards, is screened by a ragged hedge of pines and kudzu-vined sycamores. Sitting in my metal motel chair in my driveway, I can hear the golfers yelling "fore" as the sliced ball crashes into the scrub across the street. Later I see the foursome hacking through the underbrush with their clubs, looking for the lost balls. Mowing my front yard, I'll find one or two dinged up balls buried in the long grass. I keep these discoveries in a big yellow bowl on the dining room table to give to my father when he visits to play golf each winter.

2

The couple of streets of ranch homes on the hills above the golf course once must have been *the* address in Tuscaloosa. Built after the war, the neighborhood is the waking reality of a fantasy conceived in the foxholes. To be able to putter over to the club by means of your own electric cart, that was the dream. Every house has a view of the fairways rolling toward the dark river in the distance. But the money of those heady days, now, has gone, jumped north over the river to paper company land growing houses instead of trees. There, there are new country clubs with their necklaces of garden homes and McMansions hugging the shores of artificial lakes. My neighborhood is worse for wear, shabby even. Its lawns, like my own lawn, are ragged with a mixed prairie of centipede and crab grasses, creepers, ivies, and vines, the whole Southern swampy ecology that stands in contrast to the groomed swath of grass across the crumbling road.

3

My neighbors ask me what I read. They have seen me sitting in my motel chair, reading. They invite me to sit with them on their enclosed porches looking out over the golf course. We drink eight ounces of Coca-Cola served in sweating glass bottles. They all tell me that Walker Percy wrote here overlooking the country club. *Love in the Ruins* was written while visiting friends who lived in the house in the cul-de-sac at the end of the road. The golf course in that book is our golf course, they tell me.

4

Sitting in my driveway in my motel chair, I can watch the freight engine move a short string of cars through the golf course. The treble of the diesel notches up a thump or two as it leans into the hummock by the tennis courts. The spur leads from the main line downtown through the country club over to the tire plant and the refinery on the far side of the course and was built through the fairways during the war. The country club with its rail line hazard is hard by the lock and dam on the Black Warrior River, which casts a concrete backdrop to the green expanse. Tugs with tows of coal and covered barges of cement slide behind clutches of golfers skylined and foreshortened on exposed decks of the back nine tees by the river. They take practice swings as the ships blow their horns entering the locks. Off in the distance, on the other side of the river, the municipal airport launches, each morning, flights of executive jets. The paper company and Mercedes planes take off over the golf course. A pastoral: Green rolling hills. Pools of white sand. Ponds of black water. The light glints on the steel rails. The bridges of the ships slip by, visible above the green-level levees. The white jets circle, sink through the branches of the weeping trees overhead, making their evening approaches into the setting sun.

5

In the evening, the automatic sprinklers sprout sprays of water on the tees and greens. The hiss of the irrigation mixes with the saw of the cicada and the chorus of peepers in the copses. The air is warm and close. Lightning bugs rise up out of the grass.

6

One weekend soon after moving in to my house, I sit in my driveway on my motel chair reading *Love in the Ruins* when a convoy of identical electric carts, bumper to bumper, jostles by. The old men are two to a cart. Each waves at me. They wear the funny hats and gloves with straps and cut-outs. It is the start of a scramble tournament. The participants disperse to all the tees to start play simultaneously instead of launching one after another at the first hole. The motors sizzle and hum as they head up the hill and drift around the corner. Here they use the public street, but down by the ninth tee, they can slide onto the network of asphalt paths built for the carts. As the string of carts trundles past, I can see through the trees out to other convoys creeping slowly onto the back nine in the distance. It takes minutes to witness this slow parade. The clubs clank on the rough roadway. I can tell the old men are anxious, ready for the contest to come. They laugh and slap the backs of their partners, doff their hats. Then they are gone, rounding the curve by the ophthalmologist's house. After awhile, an air horn sounds down by the clubhouse, signaling the start of simultaneous play. The neighbors say they once used a shotgun, its report echoing off the concrete lock and dam.

7

My house at 29 Country Club Hills is built on fill. My lawn runs downhill to fall off into a ravine where water runs when it rains and where English ivy and Virginia creeper, poison ivy and honeysuckle boil up to entwine the cyclone fence enclosing my backyard. Where my house sits must have once been air over a wider gulch. My street crosses the ravine over a culvert that drains the water out into the golf course. On the other side of the ravine, tucked behind a little redoubt, is the clutch of buildings owned by the country club. From where I sit in my metal motel chair, I can just see the end of the corrugated metal covering the pole barn where they store the golf carts. Once, on the shady road above the culvert, a snapping turtle the size of a manhole cover lounged for an afternoon. The golf carts steered cautiously around him. At night I dream of this house washing away. When it rains, it rains tropically. The old seamed gutters of the house are clogged by pine straw. Water sheets down the driveway, the street. The red dirt turns to a red slip that glazes everything with a powdery rust.

8

Every morning, I watch my neighbor, an old woman tending her grandson, take a walk. She carries a bucket in the hand not holding the hand of the child who toddles beside her. She looks for lost balls in the rough and in the lawns of the houses adjacent to the golf course. She finds them in the piles of pine straw left curbside for the city to pick up on Mondays with the other yard debris. On the weekend she sits on the curb across the road from the ninth tee with the bucket of scrounged balls she has washed and polished and sells them to the golfers as they play through. The golfers have had a few beers by then, and they have lost a few balls that my neighbor will find tomorrow or the day after. So even though it is frowned on by the club, they buy a couple or three back from her. I see them groggily examine the balls' branding and check for the nicks and deep smiles cut in the dimpled surface before they flip their choices in the air as if to test the aerodynamics. Then they reach into their pockets.

9

On Mondays, the club is closed. There are signs tacked on the pine tree trunks bordering the course saying that what you are

x

x

looking at is private property and that there is no trespassing. Black kids from the neighborhoods next to our strip of genteel cottages ignore the signs, and each Monday morning, in foursomes themselves, lugging tackle, bait buckets, lunch baskets, and plastic pails they use as creels, they wander out onto the course. They fish the water hazards and the runoff ditches and then work their way over to the river, catching catfish mostly. At night returning, they stop to show me that day's string of fish, and tell me the story again about the alligators that once lived on the course and might live there still.

10

When I first moved to Alabama, I was asked if I played golf. Little did I know then I would find a house next to the country club. No, I told them, I don't play. That's a shame, they said, since you can play here nine months out of the year. They laughed and continued. Just not in June, July, or August. In the summer the green of the grass of the fairways is leeched away by the sun. Action on the course all but disappears. Young boys in big hats who carry, on their rounded backs, big awkward bags of jangling clubs, trudge over the bleached hills. Lessons and league play. They hit skimming shots that skip along the placid seared surface of the grass and steaming cart paths, ricocheting like stones on the mirage ponds generated by the heat. I have fled indoors. My motel chair is chilled by the air conditioning. I read a book in the living room, look up from time to time through the glaring picture window. The course shimmers through the trees.

11

Very early each morning the greenskeeper's men start their work grooming the course, changing the pin positions on the greens, raking pine straw from the bunkers. A parade of Dr. Seuss vehicles streams out from the compound of metal buildings down the road. Converted electric carts stuffed with hand tools where golfers would stow their clubs putter about. Other carts haul wagons heaped with sugar-fine sand to replenish the hazards or fill up the divots on the tees. There are sousaphone-shaped machines used to blow the leaves and bark from the fairways. There are mowers of all types, their gangly gang of twisted blades daintily suspended by means of wires and pulleys for running at full speed on the public road to get to the part of the course where yesterday they left off cutting. Later, I'll see the half-sized tractors creeping along, trailed by a train of fidgety reels V-ed behind the hitch. My favorite contraptions are the donkey motors, big engines with handle bars and their mowing decks thrust out ahead like a cow catcher. Their drivers, steering, stand behind on a tiny, almost invisible platform like the musher on a dog sled. I love the illusion of this levitation, the careless, effortlessly floating men, slaloming between the neat rows of long-leafed pine. Men, on foot nearer by, sweep the borders of the rough and the underbrush with hand implements angled like golf clubs. They swing the weed wackers, motorized scythes, as fluidly as the golfers practicing approach shots, pitches, chips. Back and forth, back and forth. The puny engines making an insect sawing. The men work their ways back to the clubhouse, the various pitches of their small engines sputtering out, the course groomed, before the first tee time.

12

The realtor showing me this house asked if I was going to join the country club. "It's very reasonable," she said. She thought its proximity was a real selling point. "I don't golf," I said. That wasn't the only thing happening at the club, she continued. She mentioned the tennis courts and the pool. "There's a new chef in the dining room, and a whole mess of folks just belong for the food." And then she wistfully recalled the dances on the terrace in the summers. And later that summer, after I moved in, I did hear the old band music drifting over from the verandas and patios. The club, she told me, was here long before the houses were built. They built the houses after the war. It was a new idea then. It was glorious. Those dances are reported in *Stars Fell on Alabama*, a book I read that first year while sitting in the driveway. Sitting in my metal chair beneath the stars, I hear the bubbles of old dance melodies down at the club. I do hear, on breezy summer weekend nights, the murmur of the dancers, the occasional guffaw, and the suggestion of chiming glass. A kind of lullaby.

13

If the weather is right, the smell of cracked oil and vulcanized rubber creeps up the valley along the river from the factories beyond the golf course. Some days it seems to have bonded chemically with the humidity, locked into the still air, and the reek lingers, impossible to get used to, a kind of aromatic film. Other days there is a just a hint, a few long strands of molecules, carbon cooking, dispersed within a breath of breeze as it freshens. Friends visiting those days stop midsentence, nostrils flaring. "Someone," they say, "must be tarring a roof somewhere." Our roofs are never tight enough. Osmosis. The smells saturate the house. Something has been left on the stove. The stove has been left on. Something is burning.

14

Sirens go off over at the club. There is sheet lightning in the distance. The golf course is crowded with players who, interrupted by the warning, reluctantly make their ways back to the clubhouse to get out of the rain. Bolts of lightning have been known to travel miles looking for the conductive synapse of a golfer, clad in metal spikes and gripping a 5 iron, to enter the ground. The rain now begins to sheet and the low ground fills immediately with the gray layers of runoff. I can see the lightning walking up the river, the green carts scurrying beneath the lowering clouds and the tendrils of sparks. A train, lit up and sounding its horn, wades through the course against the stream of carts flowing back to the club. Heaven spoiled by heaven.

15

A neighbor has told me that when George Wallace built the new courthouse downtown the rubble from the old Beaux Arts one was hauled out here and dumped into the ravine behind my house. Scattered on the floor of the gorge, covered with vines, are the remnants of capitals carved with acanthus leaves, fluted column drums, defaced faces of Justice and Law, rusting escutcheons and cracked hinges from the old wooden doors. Melting marble steps. Drifts of fragmented letters and words. Gargoyles sunk in the mud. I can't get up the nerve to work my way down into there, though I think about it often. Perhaps my neighbor is fooling with me. Through the links of my chain-link fence I peer into the jungle canopy that roils up out of the ravine. Nothing and everything.

16

In the winter, the grounds crew stacks canvas tarps on wooden pallets next to the greens. On the nights there might be a freeze, they spread out the tarps on the greens to protect the grass. In the morning, the canvases are white with frost, the fabric stiff from the cold, frozen in undulating waves, a meringue. In the morning, as the sun warms the course, the crew folds up the tarps again, revealing the brilliant green greens in their organic organ shapes set in the still frost-white fairways. The crew goes from one hole to the next, the first foursomes playing patiently behind them.

17

A deer came with the house. It is life-sized and painted. Over the years its cement flesh has rotted. The iron tendon of its rear leg is exposed and rusted. The velvet of his antlers has worn away, leaving the branches of corroded rebar. In the spring and summer the deer is enveloped by the creepers and vines that clad him in a kind of topiary coat he sheds in fall. His flat, staring eye fixes on me as I lounge in my metal chair in the driveway. The deer seems alive because the foliage around him is alive. He seems to move since the setting he poses in transforms day to day. Or maybe he is moving. He is being tugged on by the ivy, bullied by the tendrils, slightly shifted over time, sifting into the forest behind him. A visitor will be surprised, mistake the deer for a real deer surprised by the visitor. I watch them watch each other. Both hold perfectly still, waiting for the other's next move.

18

Through the picture window, I can see through the trees to the ninth green where golfers in pastel outfits and oversized hats take turns putting. Behind me is another vista. The long wall of the living room is wallpapered with a mural which depicts, in three colors, an elegant antebellum mansion set on a rolling plantation sward. The edges of the house are smudged by ivy and draped with wisteria. The weeping trees are bearded with moss. There are no people in the picture, so it is hard to say whether the picture represents a ruin or not. It attempts to capture, I think, in its gestural, impressionistic style the indigenous Romantic nostalgia which hereabouts is so deeply layered. You would think the wallpaper is just another example of that longing. But look closer. It's easy to miss. In the front lawn of the ancient house is the green puddle of a putting green and in its center a vertical brush stroke which, at first, you thought was meant to be a sapling or an indication of the breeze, but now on closer inspection turns out to be a pin, its checkered flag snapping in an invisible wind.

What I Want to Tell

A SEQUENCE OF ROOMS

A Room

"What do you want to tell me?" Doctor X asks me. I am in an office room, an office room very much like my own office room. It has a desk, a desk chair, and some chairs. The overhead lights, a panel in the false drop ceiling, are off. The desk lamp is on as is a torchiere in the corner, its halogen humming in the silence that follows the question. What light there is sifts through a drawn blind on the window. When I moved to S four years ago, I looked up the city in the places-rated guides and found it ranked first in only one category. S, with its month or so of scattered days of available sunlight, days bright enough to cast one's shadow on the ground, is the only place to live if one wishes to avoid skin cancer. The city is famous for its cold as well. I want to tell him about when I moved to town what a colleague wrote on the title page of his book when he autographed it for me. "Welcome to S," he told me. "With warm regards, W. P.S., You're going to need all the warmth you can get!"

The Same Room

"What do you want to tell me?" I find the question hysterically hilarious but not so as the man who asked me, Doctor X, would know. In a word, I am depressed. I think of that word, depressed, as one of his words. My words have yet to arrive. He doesn't know a thing about me yet as I haven't told him a thing, and I am sitting stone still in his office thinking about what I have to tell him and how funny that is since what I have to tell him is about telling. For the last twenty years, I have made a living, more or less, telling stories, always imagining an imaginary audience prompting me to tell a story with a question like this. And I have been teaching students the last twenty years, telling them how to tell stories. And now the last year and a half I have been telling the same story about something that happened a year and a half ago, to a variety of people—investigative committees, administrators, colleagues, reporters, hearing examiners, students, friends who have called. And every time I tell the story of the thing that happened a year and a half ago, that occasion of the new telling, that version of me telling the story and the way I told it that particular time, becomes attached to the bigger story, the ongoing story, so that each time I tell the story there is more of it to tell, and when I am rehearsing the story for someone new, as I am about to do now for Doctor X, I am also not simply telling the story but paying attention to myself telling the story so that the next time I tell it I will remember to add the details of the last time I told the story, the way the room was, its light and furnishings and the person or persons there, so that those things can be incorporated into the next time I tell the story.

Still in the Same Room

What is so funny is that I have, with great authority, told my students all about where to start a story, even using Latin to give it a special patina of power. *In medias res*. In the middle of things. I tell my students of this ancient technique. How to go backwards from there in order to go forward. Funny, then, that I have started here in this room, in the middle of things, to tell the story again, this time to you who are reading this story. Funny, too, that when I was in the doctor's office and when he asked me the question "What do you want to tell me?" I, a person who makes a living, more or less, telling stories and teaching other people how to tell stories, was silenced for the moment by the existential nature of the task. That is, that we must tell stories in some order since our words line up one after another and accumulate and are read here in a conventional sequence from the top down, from left to right, are followed step by step. Now, I am in this room because I am at the end of one rope of words. I wish at this moment I could tell the doctor what I have to tell all at once, simultaneously. Though it is true that the events that have led me here happened in a sequence, so much of the sequence now seems repetitive, glossed, as if I have been polishing a table and a flat surface has taken on this depth. Rooms within rooms. I sit there. It is like a pen held to paper, this story I have to tell, the stain of ink spreading, the color deepening everywhere all at once. And I have no words, no means to make them tell. Not a line at all. A dark blot spreading.

Another Room (Versions)

I am not in this room. It is the end of March and dark. A party at a student's house. A poet, D, in my department, drunk, calls a woman—not his student but a student in the department—a name and throws a drink in her face. Subsequent retellings of the events of that night would add detail, more or less, because the people there were poets and fiction writers, narrators all. It was night and dark. There was a visiting poet who later, back home in Idaho during the investigation, refused to ever tell his story. Versions vary but some say he said or didn't say something about the woman's breasts or D said or didn't say something about her breasts to the visiting poet or to the woman. Which did or didn't spark the woman to say something or not to D who was either hurt or mad by what was said or not said. He threw the drink and the liquid hit the woman, everyone agrees. But there are versions about what was said by D, the words delivered with the gesture in the air with the alcohol. I was struck later, on April Fool's Day, when I heard a version of the events for the first time by phone along with the news that the student had filed a complaint of sexual harassment with the university, by the gesture itself. I was struck by the gesture itself, the throwing of a drink. How artificial it seemed. How like something self-consciously cribbed from a movie. The words that were, or, perhaps, were not uttered, how they seemed, even then, the first time I heard them, so scripted and rehearsed. And I thought of Henry James, the great chronicler of the tragedy of the broken teacup, who wrote that stories reveal themselves through selected perception and amplification.

An Amplification

The room where I teach my workshops at the university in S has been renovated. In this old building the high-ceilinged rooms have been cut in two and the floor of the room I am in now floats halfway up the old space. The tops of the old windows, then, arch frowning at our feet. Outside it is gray and cold. What light there is must struggle up, reflected from the dark ground and the stone pavement outside. We talk about the two-step formula of how one gets a story started. There is the "Once upon a time" and there is the "One day." The anecdotal "Once upon a time" seems easy for my students. They understand the chronic tensions of life, the conflicts of family, friends, lovers. They sense the asymmetry of character strengths and weaknesses, the pressures of job and gender, history and place. They know the atmospheric weight of birth and death and the specific gravity of a character's attraction or repulsion. This they get. This they get because it seems like life, the elaboration of conflict, tension, and difference. Life is like this. What is hard is the "One day." What is hard is the making up of the "One day," the thing that happens that sets all of these accumulated and congested details into motion so that more happens. That is the fiction part of fiction I tell them, that is the thing that you make up. It is a coincidence, I tell them, that one day the magic mirror tells the evil queen that she is no longer the fairest in the land. Coincidences like this we accept *in stories*. I tell them that these coincidences are what make anecdotes stories because the "One day" allows for things to change. Our lives are a systemic melodramatic mess, busy but static. The "One day" is hard to imagine, but this is the part that must be imagined. This "One day" that changes your life. We shake our heads in sympathy with one another. How hard this will be to imagine I tell them reassuringly. How the "One day" has always been not life but the hard part of the art, the artifice of art. And then, one day, a man at a party throws a drink at a woman . . .

The First Room

But that is not what I want to tell Doctor X in his office when he asks me what I want to tell him. It is now the fall after the party at the end of March where D has thrown the drink, and much has happened. This, the following list of events, is still happening in my head. There is the meeting in W's office with some of the other faculty of the creative writing program where K and H and I talk about what we should do. There is the meeting in my office with the woman who was hit by the drink. And the meeting with the chairman of the department and the faculty members who make up an executive committee in the committee room with its big table, the same room where I used to teach my fiction writing classes. And this is about the time of the meeting before what I call the big meeting, where the creative writing faculty meets to decide whether we should have the big meeting. Then there is the big meeting with the open mikes and the reading of statements. And then, after that, all the small private meetings with individual students who, because of what went on with the big meeting, now have things to say about D and the program in creative writing. And this is before the investigative hearings by the faculty senate in another committee room. The meeting with the graduate students in creative writing I call the blizzard meeting because I made a reference to a late-spring snowstorm that was going on as we met, the wet snow turning the tiny windows in the room white. The meeting at the Thai restaurant and at the bar before. Then, after the report came out listing D's history of behavior but also the program's complacency and complicit nature. The meeting in the vice president's office where W, K, and H, the other writers in the program, denounced the whole investigation. The meeting in the office of the chairman of the investigative committee when I gave him a memo that made clear how I differed from W, K, and H about what should be done. Then the actual hearing itself where I testified in a room to a committee. The committee sat with its back to windows and I remember the sky being occluded as always, but it was summer then, June, and it might have been one of the bright blue skies worth remembering if I could remember it. D was sitting next to me on the left and the woman who brought the charges on the right. A committee member asks me, "Given all that was going on in your program why didn't you do something?" And I say, "This is what I am doing. I am doing this now." And I could start with that or with the summer writers' conference two weeks later where I am on the staff with D who hears, that week, the results of the hearing and leaves early and where I hear from the new chair of the English department that the other teachers of creative writing, W, K, and H, now are angry at me. But I didn't start in any of these places. I started at the meeting that happens later that summer where I sit for five hours and listen to W, K, and H angrily tell their stories about me and, afterwards, in an office very much like mine, I weep for two hours more, not only because what they have said about me has hurt but because I know that the things they have said have been designed to hurt, and I realize that I need help. I need a way to stop telling the story of these stories. The meetings in meetings. I need, I understand, a story that would no longer nest in a nest of other stories.

An Amplification

Crying is funny. I am holding on to the arms of the office chair I am in, howling. Every time I come up for air, I am conscious of the secretaries outside this office at their desks in the outer office. Surely they can hear these noises, these sounds I am making. The gagging. The sputtering. The hiccups of breath. The empty whoops. The plosive sighs. They must hear this on the other side of the glass wall and hollow-cored door. Filtered I could sound like a Stooge whose own comic sound effects accompanies his beating. Two friends are holding me down, it seems, in the chair. I let them touch me. I want them to touch me. And they are making sounds too, a kind of burbling murmur that comforts me when I hear it and initiates a whole new burst of wailing in me, hearing it, out of gratitude. I have no words but this slurry of speech. I am way beyond words in this place. I am letting go. Perhaps that is why I am clinging so hard to the arms of this office chair, why my friends have collapsed across my knees, wrapped their arms around my shoulders. It is as if I would levitate on all the unsounded breath I am gulping. I believe I am communicating that, for a while here in this office, I don't want to talk anymore. I have come here after five hours in a room in the philosophy department. At this moment, I am remembering just one sliver of what went on. I remember H instructing me on my attitude, my manner, the way I choose my words. He says I have, on occasion, been sarcastic, then defines the word for me, its roots, as the ripping of flesh. When I was a student, a teacher told me that humans use language to convey only one message. "Do you like me? Do you like me? Like me!" I remember laughing when I heard this for the first time, a kind of witty distillation of experience teachers deliver in a classroom and that passes and is passed along as a truth.

A Room in the Philosophy Department

In August, the chair of the English department arranges a meeting with a professional mediator. It is held on the top floor of my building, where one wall is all windows looking out over the hazy sky. Off in the distance I can see what everyone says, quite proudly, is the most polluted lake in the Western Hemisphere. I didn't want to meet again. I sensed what was coming. But the chair assures me the mediator is a pro and will be fair. I walk last into the room in the philosophy department and notice that the table where W, K, and H sit is sown with mini Hershey bars the mediator is encouraging us to eat. As I recount this detail, Doctor X snorts. And I tell him the mediator says that chocolate will relax us. I continue my story about the meeting in a room of the philosophy department. I realize the mediator with her big felt pens and clipboards and xeroxed ground rules about "no piling on" is not anticipating the meeting for which I know we have met. She is attempting to manage a group of angry, professionally verbal people with chocolate and chalk. W's most recent book about the trauma of his experience in Vietnam will be a National Book Award finalist. K's new memoir of her childhood will soon be on the best-seller list. Between us I count a couple dozen books and a half century of classroom teaching. The mediator, according to her resume, has authored articles entitled "Teambuilding in a Technical Environment" and "Using Psychology to Reward Teamwork." In her report written after the meeting, she writes that the bad feelings will dissipate. Like the weather, I think. In W's boyhood memoir, the one he autographed for me with warm regards, there is a scene where his evil stepfather sadistically makes him clean out every bit of mustard from an empty jar W threw away. The stepfather twists the jar into W's eye. Is it empty? I call this meeting, the meeting in August in a room in the philosophy department, the Mustard Meeting. We are going to get every bit of mustard. We play along with the mediator a while. I look out the window. The lake. The clouds. K, impatient, says to W, ignoring the mediator who never speaks again, "Do you want me to start or do you want to?" He wants to.

The Waiting Room

This is nothing. I know this is nothing compared to what has happened to other people, what is happening to people now, what is happening to the people here, say, in Doctor X's waiting room. It is nothing in comparison. It wasn't bodily trauma in any way. I am not physically ill. I am not dying. Nor have I struck anyone. I do not feel like striking anyone. This is about something that happened at work, I keep telling myself, something that is now way out of proportion. What happened finally, I think, was I couldn't fix things when I thought I could. I thought things could be fixed. Or I thought things needed fixing. Something. It occurs to me, in the waiting room, that since last March I have been sitting in my office listening to students and colleagues tell me stories about the consequences of D's actions and being helpless, really. How do I feel in the waiting room? Embarrassed. Embarrassed that I am so stunned by this nothing. Embarrassed that I have hired a professional listener to listen to my tale. And I am taken by the luxuriousness of this, of hiring an audience, this utter indulgence. I am depressed, depressed with a small D. To me, the depression is a kind of small black dot, a dot no bigger than the period at the end of the sentence, at once an insubstantial speck of ink while at the same time a collapsed world with the specific gravity of a black hole. I am taken by this paradox. I am insisting too much on this nothing. What has happened is, in my professional opinion, boring, yet I am deeply fascinated with the intricacies of the events. The storyteller in me keeps telling me there is no story here, really. But I can't stop wanting to make it a story. I can't stop telling it. This is nothing but it has become everything. By calling it nothing I can't rid myself of it. And I am quite conscious of the inconsequence of all this to others. They see it as the nothing it is. They suggest, politely, at the end of another rendition that I talk to someone. And here I am. Here I am ready to tell this story again.

A Room in a Basement of a Church

In the middle of things, a friend takes me to an open AA meeting. He suggests that, though I don't drink, alcohol in this crisis has profoundly changed my life. D was drunk when he threw the drink, and he did throw a *drink*, and has offered that he was drunk as a mitigating circumstance and has indicated that he has entered the program. He is sober now, he says. A changed man. The room in the basement of the church feels, oddly, like my classroom where stories are told, tables and chairs, but it is not like my classroom. The framing of the storytelling is different. And my friend who is a literary scholar tips me as to the aesthetic differences to come. He tells his story to us without the literary flourish I know he knows. He has told me that the notions of creativity and originality are different in this room. The stories are *supposed* to be repetitious and predictable. And they are. They are relentless in this relentless style, their stylelessness. That's the point. The One Day here does not lead to a rising action, climax, and denouement but to the next one day and the next.

In Camera

After another day of meetings, I sit in the living room, the answering machine on, screening calls. My wife and I watch television and, during the commercials, I rehearse for her the scrolling events at school. The phone rings, and we both start. We hear an angry voice laying down a track on the tape. New threats and curses. An aggressive gloss of the very version of events I have just related to my wife. All night, every night, for months, voices emanating from the machine. "Talk to me, you sorry son of a bitch" or "Call me, I've got something to say to you." The little box of the TV we watch seems to have only one story to tell. Scandal and corruption everywhere it seems. The detective stories, all the investigations only reveal ambiguous evidence. Locally, the story I am involved in disappears in the local news as another sexual harassment investigation blooms at the nearby airbase. Men and women fighter pilots fighting. My wife and I, everyone I know, longs, I think, for an actual dogfight. The gray jets screaming and looping in the gray skies above the city of S. Instead there are the usual waves of statements and denials, charges and counter-charges issued for the press with or without attribution. The whole catastrophe. Behind the stock footage of the F-16s skidding down the runway in the late-season snowstorm, I imagine the G-suited pilots in the cockpit of their offices, the warrens of their bureaus, the meetings and workshops, the sessions with consultants. It is the season of debriefing. And I imagine that cast of characters in their own living rooms watching this broadcast, the one I am watching, listening to this endless reel unraveling, taken from the wreckage, the black box of this crash that keeps crashing.

Another Amplification

For years I have been routinely sketching for my students the theory of realistic fiction, the one that ties fiction to the rise of the middle class and the invention of privacy and leisure. There is time now, I suggest, to read books and there are places now where one can go to read them. And the content of domestic fiction? This reiteration: Intimates keep secrets from one another. The drama is in the discovery of those secrets and the discovery of the depth of those secrets. Adultery, a favorite theme. The metaphoric exhaustion of an upstairs and down. The closets that are rooms within rooms. Could Freud have even evolved his theories without the elaboration of all the specialized rooms within the detached house? The bathroom! The bedroom! The innovation of the hallway was profound, I say. No more walking through rooms to get to other rooms. Doors can be closed in order that secret things go on behind them. I see my students roll their eyes. This is all theory, I say, laughing, this storytelling that takes place within walls that turn transparent, that is about the renovation of the chambered spaces of the house and the heart and the head.

In the Room

I want to tell him everything but there isn't enough time. That's not it exactly. There isn't enough space either. I can only provide a map of this disaster and the scale will always be distorted, will not correspond point to point. You can't feel what I feel. I tell him this. And I tell him this: How hard this is to tell. And I muse for a moment about such a map, a map on the scale of 1:1, a map that when unfolded would map everything exactly. The map would settle on those chairs, the desk, on us exactly, a new skin, would correspond exactly molecule to molecule. You would feel what I feel. I have run out of words. I look around for another handy metaphor, another physical tool to pry open all the abstractions. Any port in the storm. It is the place, I suggest, that has made me so sad. This particular combination of physical detail. Maybe it's in the water, the air. It is always so cold and so dark. We both look at the window, and Doctor X draws open the blinds dramatically. The lumens in the room increase infinitesimally. We regard the familiar gray sky, the light my wife jokes about each morning. The famous light, she says, painters come here from the whole world over to capture.

A Final Amplification

I edited a magazine once called *Poet&Critic*, and, as part of a promotion campaign, I ran a contest for a poster design to feature the words POET and CRITIC. I received fifty entries, and all but one characterized POET in a display font that was flowery and fluid, italic at the very least, but always cast to look improvisational, spontaneous, creative. The CRITIC, on the other hand, was figured as severe, in serifed types or bold block letters, regimented and defined. Only one designer reversed this take—the POET permanent and the CRITIC scribbled in by hand. And that was right. That was it exactly. All the stories I have read, all the books and magazines and typescripts—these were printed, *set* in type. It is my scrawl of analysis, my random thoughts, the critic in the margin and between the lines, the editor that ferrets around by hand amending commentary. It is so difficult to see the obvious. I watch Doctor X scribble on a pad of yellow legal paper as I talk. I tell him about a story I read once. The story was about Superman, the comic book hero, but it was a pop treatment. The author's trick was to take the conventions of the form and the character to logical conclusions. When Superman, in this story, uses his X-ray vision, I tell Doctor X, all he sees is lead. The X-ray keeps going, see, through everything until it can't go through anything more, until it runs into some lead. And in this story, I say, Superman's speech balloons and his bubbles of thoughts are invulnerable like the rest of him. He says something or he thinks something and the words appear for a second above his head and then they drift down, coating him in verbiage, a kind of sticky paste, layer after layer, impervious to detergent or thinner. Our hero encased in a cocoon of words, the light filtered by the thatch of entwined letters.

In the Waiting Room

"You can go," Doctor X says. I am in his office and I take his "you can go" both ways. That is, I can go now and leave this room which is, I realize at this instant, a kind of waiting room now, outside, as it is, of the next room I must enter. Or I can go, leave this place, this S, altogether. There was a moment in the Mustard Meeting, in the room in the philosophy department, a moment when I knew I would go. With the silent mediator opening square after square of chocolate, enthralled by the stories being constructed by W, K, and H. In the middle of this, I was struck by the thought that all was lost, that I was lost. I was an M. I was merely a character now in this room, in this place, written out in the meantime, in the corroborating narratives of W, K, and H, reiterated in the meetings they had together in the run-up to this meeting with me. An M. An M who had been written up and written off. I wasn't in that room anymore. So I could go. And I went.

The Copy Room

I am in the copy room, copying my vita, an academic resume. The copy room is windowless, air forced in through vents near the ceiling. The wall of shelves is stacked with reams of white paper, letter and business. The lights hum and the copier stutters through its cycle. All around are the fossil remains of extinct business machines, heaps of the obsolete technologies of duplication—thermograph, ditto, mimeo—their cords coiled. The machines are clad in those exhausted colors—putty, gunmetal, drab. With each swipe it makes, the green light of the copy machine leaks a little from beneath the lid. For the purposes of furthering my employment opportunities elsewhere, I have reduced my life to a page of copy. I am making fifty copies of the copy. The vita's form is boilerplate. There are bullet heads for EDUCATION, AWARDS, PUBLICATIONS, TEACHING, SERVICE, in bold all caps. H comes into the copy room, queuing up behind me. We exchange pleasantries. "Be done in a jif." We have all been pleasant this fall after we have CLEARED THE AIR in the August meeting, the one I call the Mustard Meeting. That's how W, K, and H characterize what happened then and there: THE AIR WAS CLEARED. WE CLEARED THE AIR. On my vita, there is the bullet labeled EXPERIENCE, and I have advertised there the position I still hold, Director of Creative Writing. The meeting in August, the one I call the Mustard Meeting, was held because W, K, and H had LOST CONFIDENCE in me as Director. Now a few weeks later I am still Director. "Be the Director," I was told at the end of the Mustard Meeting. You know, Doctor X says to me in his office, this hasn't been about you as Director. This hasn't been about CLEARING THE AIR. This hasn't been about LOSS OF CONFIDENCE. The copy machine performs its little rumba of reproduction, counting down to naught.

The Cloud Room

Before we go out to the car to go for good, we walk through the empty house in S, my wife and I and our two boys. We say goodbye to all the empty rooms, starting in the basement where Sam had set some handprints on a jacking pad we'd poured when we moved in. I carry the little one, Nick, the two year old, and borrow the chant from one of his bedtime story books. I have learned, in telling my stories to Doctor X, in listening to myself tell my stories to Doctor X, the power of litany to both cudgel and comfort. At this moment, I am all for the possibility of comfort, the soothing murmur of the lullaby, of language laying to rest. Say good-bye, I say. Good-bye kitchen. Good-bye dining room, good-bye. Good-bye living room. Good-bye stairs. Good-bye your room and good-bye Sam's room. Good-bye our room.

Good-bye bathroom. Good-bye Mom's office painted school bus yellow. We climb into the finished attic where some sorry soul poked a few skylights through the roof to get what sun there was, my office, where I wrote, three stories up inside a blue house. The cloud room, Sam called it when he first saw it. Dad is in the cloud room. Say, good-bye cloud room, good-bye.

Going Up

1

I am a gawker. A bumpkin, a hayseed from the Midwest, I stand on the wide sidewalks of cities to look up at the tall buildings. The pedestrians stream grudgingly by, parting into channels on either side of my shoal-like stillness. The walls launch from the same concrete on which I am standing. They vault into the air. This looking creates pleasant illusions. My vision, as it swipes along the lithic or glass facades, recreates the sped-up record of the tower's construction, brick on brick furiously morphing into a solid sheet, raining upward. It is that cinematic technique of vertigo, that pulled focus of the camera lens, the simultaneous clarity of the very close and the brilliant detail of distance itself stretching, stretching even further away. I am looking straight up! All that is square to the solid deck beneath my feet, all these truly true vertical lines, diminishing as they go (and they do go), vector toward that very center of the endless sky. All lines point to the vanishing point. I am looking *straight* up! I can see the point of vanishing. This perfect lesson of perspective. This gawking is, perhaps, a function of my midwestern-ness, an expression of my eyes' evolution on a flat plain. The horizon is all periphery, one endless sentence. The horizon is not this concentrated speck of attention up there, not this black pinprick of convergence, not this dot at the end of seeing seeing, not this infinite period.

2

They *are* called cars. The first one I remember was piloted, its operator uniformed identically to the then contemporary, early '60s stewardess. The white gloves. The fitted flannel suit. The military buttons. The raked hat with affixed winged device and contrasting piping edging its many folds. Now elevators are self-service, and we forget because they are designed to make us forget, that they are vehicles moving through space. The hobbled acceleration of that motion, today, is so damped, disguised. You enter. The doors close. The doors open. And you are somewhere else. It's as if the building rearranged itself outside while you waited in the closed box, or burly work crews struck the lobby like a stage set behind the sliding curtain. Sure, the numbers flash as you pass from floor to floor but that is simple distraction, the only real movement this awkward analog one. My first trip? The first one I remember. I traveled from the ground to the third floor of a small department store. The operator manipulated levers, turned wheels guiding our vehicle. She stopped at the intervening floors, the stool she leaned on springing back up against the wall as she reached across the car to open the first set of double doors. "Going up. Mezzanine. Going up. First floor." The landings were never exact, the floor of the car and the floor of the floor misaligned like a square of sidewalk dislodged by a tree root. She inched the two floors together, the nudge teasing the tension in the cables to sing, covering her operations with recitation of the floor's merchandise, a kind of tour guide. "Watch your step." Later, I waited on the third floor. I was in another world, the world of underwear, husky pants, school shoes, brownie uniforms, belts, handkerchiefs, flatware, china, lunch pails, luggage, and travel alarms. But I lingered at the landing. I watched the cars arrive from below, depart. There were two shafts, the cars' alternating rise and fall, a kind of breathing. A distinct shadow filled the squares of light in the opaque windows of the outer doors. The bell struck flat, the tinny ceremony of arrival. "Watch your step." I made no move for the empty car.

"Going down." The doors slid shut. The muffled announcement of the next destination filtered through. I watched the shadow sink, compress into a line at the lip of the floor. Going, then gone.

3

Z is the other axis of travel. When we travel, we think in terms of going north, going south, even thinking of that as going up or down, the three dimensions of our world constantly flattened to the two of our maps. We laugh at the flat earth notion but we operate happily within it. Altitude, the forgotten coordinate of place, escapes us when latitude and longitude will suffice as we roam our vast world and report on our extended movements around it. Even when a journey considers ascent, to climb a mountain, say, there is the usual flat travel to that place. The scramble to the summit is always described as a sprint, the last burst of energy, an afterthought, really, to the sea-level preparations and the establishment of base camps. The destination of "up" is often too foreign, too strange to be considered travel. The mountains we want to climb could be near Kathmandu, on a spine of granite in the middle of Patagonia, but even these ends of the earth can begin to seem familiar in the way the roofs of the world never do. And that strange and final frontier overhead is not even that far away. A handful of miles, the distance of a daily horizontal commute, takes you to the edge of space. A few hundred feet and you are easily on your way out of this earthbound world.

4

A few steps take you around the observation deck of the Lincoln Tower. It is a kind of trench, this little walkway of a few yards circling the building's ultimate structure, the housing for the revolving searchlight topped by the flagpole and its snapping flag. The solid wall is shoulder-high to an adult. Kids would need to be hoisted up to the shoulders of adults to see out over the wall. The tower is nineteen stories, and was once, when it was built in 1930, the tallest building in the state. It was a scale model of the Empire State Building, finished about the same time. Everything appeared quarter-sized. You can't see down. Seeing down is one of the reasons for traveling up. The looking down is a rare perspective. But the construction of the Lincoln Tower's observation deck makes it impossible to look down on the people walking below, the cars inching along the street. Instead, you must look out from the lookout. See the flat horizon, all 360 degrees of it. I used to walk the trench around the top of the Lincoln Tower gazing in all directions. Such venues often label the vantage points with the number of states, counties, miles your vision can collect. There, the sign reads, is Ohio, but it looks all the same. The green carpet of the canopy of trees, the ground fog of haze, the descending blue sky turning white. Is there a hint of the curve of the earth? Today, the Lincoln Tower is hemmed in by newer, taller buildings. The Fort Wayne Bank Building. The gas company's skyscraper. The phone company's microwave tower. The Lincoln Tower management has tilted up the searchlight's angle so the beam won't paint the windows of the offices yards away. You can see people in those adjacent structures, moving between offices, talking on the phone, eating lunch. They ignore the view mostly, or they have grown used to it. When it gets crowded in the sky, it seems as if everyone is floating. The towers are glass, transparent. You can't see the roots of the buildings. Occasionally, someone will be looking out. A man sitting at his desk, wearing a white shirt and tie, will be looking out at you, on the deck below, looking back at him. Even more rarely, several people will be looking at you simultaneously. They are all on different floors, on different parts of their different floors, a tic-tac-toe pattern. You wave, and they all wave back.

5

For a while there, Hyatt Hotels were notorious for hollowing out their buildings' center, creating the atrium lobbies that reached all the way up to the skylit roofs. The guest rooms emptied out onto terraces of balconies, suspended bridges, floating walkways with transparent floors looking down to the lobby levels, the bar there floating on an island in the middle of a pool. Often, trailing plants, bred to thrive on the filtered light and thin air, planted in the crannies and crags of the canyon wall, launched their viny tendrils into space in cascading falls of pale green foliage. The greenery softened the Escher-like angles of the vaulting geometry, aged the scalloped setbacks into ancient hanging gardens, Mayan ruins uncovered in a jungle. The elevators for reaching the upper floors became kinetic sculpture. The architects removed three walls of the elevators' shafts and walled the cars in glass outlined in strings of tiny lights. The effect, from a distance, was of these opalescent limpid creatures inching up and down a matte black aquarium wall or of these dewy drops of light scaling a slender ascending central pier of gliding gilded cables. These hotels were fortresses, blockhouses turned away from the decaying host cities outside. They were designed as refuges, as destinations in and of themselves. They packaged space. That was the most valuable part of the real estate, after all, not the footprint but the air rights. You bought the absence, the hollow, the nothing, the endless up. For this reason, their entryways were hidden, guarded, disguised. From the streets outside the facades of these cored castles were curtain walls of solid red brick, their outer windows, if they had them, were mere slits. The guest, arriving, made his way past the baffles and tunnels of the entry, finally out into these airy atriums. The heart leaped up. Here, at last, was a city of the future, a city under glass. Here, even gravity was revoked. You floated up to your room, a room wedged onto its own tier of drifting clouds.

6

My father worked as a switchman for the phone company. There was a five-story turret on the roof of the main office building downtown. The turret was the microwave tower. He would sneak me up there. The tower wasn't the familiar lacy truss of criss-crossing struts. This tower had been sheathed, for some reason, with sheets of corrugated metal painted the gray of battleships. Near the top were two decks for the white microwave collectors and transmitters. They looked like ears, of course, listening to the buzz in the air. Housed in this unusual structure they also looked, when I thought about it, like gigantic fungi, mushrooms scalloped on the bark of a tree. They hummed below us when my father took me to the top. In every direction, off in the distance, I could see the other microwave towers, the next nodes of the network. On each the white sails of its antennae cocked back toward our tower. I did think of it as a net, this invisible grid of electromagnetic impulse stitching the distance together. Off to the north, the high ground of my town, was the forest of transmission towers. The television and radio stations, a baker's dozen of the slender spires, were arranged on the horizon. All of them had the pulsing red warning lights, all on their own sequence. The tallest, because it was the tallest, also had a white strobe light. Every few seconds this explosion of light, like the radiation emanating from the tower on the old RKO Radio Picture logo, flashed out its bright bubble of energy. I think we mostly forget about these towers the way we forget about all the wires that circulate above our heads. Electric. Telephonic. The pipelines of data. We are so earthbound. We forget to notice this strata of travel. We actually go places on this plane. There, our voices carry. There, our images stream like choirs of angels on a bright ring of this elevated ether. It is only when you do physically get above this above that you see the airy layer of connection. The towers talk to one another, winking back and forth over the distance, over and over.

7

I like to call home from the tops of tall buildings. There always seem to be banks of pay phones on observation decks. "Guess where I am," I say. My parents never guess. I always say, "I think I can see your house," no matter where I am. I tell them what I can see. What states the sign says I can see. I tell them about the other tall buildings cropping up around me. I tell them about the radio stations on the observation deck. There are often radio stations. I tell them all the things I can see hidden—things hidden from below—on all the surrounding roofs. The water towers, the air conditioners with their slow-turning blades, the housings for the elevators, the skylights, the helipads. Phone calls from the tops of tall buildings are like postcards—compressed, tenuous, transmitted with a view. Thinking of you. And come to think of it, the brain is lodged on the observation floor of the body. Our thoughts peek out like so many tourists gazing from the windows in the Statue of Liberty's crown. Traveling up is a meditation. Being up is reflection. See your face reflected in the window through which you observe. What else to do but look. Look at the looking going on. Observation decks are most often hushed. If they are enclosed, there is no other sensation but sight. I begin to feel I am looking out of my body like I am looking out of the building. The world below begins to fit together as I gaze. I can see the way it fits together. That world becomes like a map; it begins to make sense like a map. To hover over it like this is to simulate the vantage of a map. Traveling up actually changes the scale of my vision. The people look like ants. Why go but to get this other angle on things? My head, yes, in the clouds.

8

There I was on the observation deck of the Sears Tower when it was the tallest building in the world. I was on the phone calling home. A cloudless day. The blue of the lake met the blue of the sky above like two swatches of paint sample, a minute modulation of the base tint separating them, blue one and blue two. A flock of crows launched from the green sward of Grant Park. As they rose the black birds transmuted, compressed and stretched into helicopters climbing. Four or five of them rising, rising up to my eye level where the two lead aircraft stalled and hovered in silence, their crew doors open and men inside looking back out at me. The tails of the hovering craft turned in circles as the others rushed past the windows, nose down, their blades pitched and biting in, the wash from their rotors beating the windows. Gone. Then those left, still levitating, drifted lazily straight up out of sight, gyring in the updraft of the building. A voice in my ear told me it was the president leaving town.

9

My little dictionary suggests that "story," the second meaning of the word—the complete horizontal division of a building constituting the area between two adjacent levels—comes to us from the Medieval Latin *historia*, "picture story." "Probably," the dictionary muses "from painted windows or sculpture on the front of buildings. See HISTORY." Indeed. I like this accident of history that abuts a synonym for floors in a building with "an account or recital of events or series of events, either true or fictitious." It conjectures a whole culture of gawkers staring up at the new buildings, getting the news from the stained glass, the bas relief, the metopes tucked under the eves. The other story, the narrative one, is said to have a rising action, its pinnacle climax and its falling off. To travel vertically is to actually feel the feel of gravity, the rush of blood to your feet on a lift, the G in your seat in the airplane. And only then the hint of weightlessness at the peak when all that's solid vectors off as you descend. There is also the experience of the other weight we take for granted, the bearing down of all that's invisible, the mass of air that isn't there until you peel through its layers and its piercing registers in your ears. John Barth calls plot an incremental perturbation, a disturbance of gravity. Sure, the borders one crosses when one travels horizontally are real. They are cultural, national. You move from one dialect to the next, one language to another. But this journey is more picaresque perhaps, mere adventures. Traveling up and quickly, it is always quickly, one transgresses frontiers not of difference but of our very physical adaptation. The air thins. The blood boils. The story of Babel is the story of the invention of babble.

10

The story goes that a camera was found in the rubble of the collapsed World Trade Center. The disc inside the camera has miraculously survived and the image that arrives via e-mail, you are told, is only the most remarkable of the many recovered. From that image, you can imagine the story behind its taking. The camera's owner and a friend are on the tower's observation deck. "Stand over there and let me get a shot of you and the city below." You see a young man, smiling broadly in the foreground. Spread out behind him and below him is the grand canyon of the metropolis, the buttes and plateaus of lower Manhattan, the glinting river, and the escarpment of New Jersey. In the near background you can see the lip of the tower itself, the observation platform elevated and set back on the roof of the building. There, a few stories below, captured digitally, is the silver fuselage of the first plane a few meters away, it seems, from that morning's first catastrophe. The picture stands for the moment before the moment things all changed. It's a hoax, of course. The debunkers point out that even if you could believe the survival of the camera within the destruction, the deck hadn't yet opened that morning. I suppose too that an electronic camera would have time-coded the image and the real moment of its composition would have been recoverable. Still. It is the stillness of the shot that transfixes the viewer. Strangely, I want it to be real. Here would be Zeno's paradox. That airplane can never transverse the infinite and infinite regressing distances between points A and B. It never happened. The subject of the photograph, the smiling young man, is looking up at the camera. He looks like he doesn't know what is about to happen. How could he? When this picture was really taken, the one that was photoshopped into the fake, it was days or weeks before the events of September 11. His innocence is so convincing. What would be the other shots on *that* disk? The routine record of observing. The panoramic view of the island. The river widening out to the sea. The minute Statue of Liberty, a paperweight, on its slip of an island. The crowd of tourists on the observation deck, many of them taking pictures of what they had seen, proof they had been there stunned by this ordinary, this uneventful day.

11

Actors say they "go up" when they forget their lines during a performance. "He is going up." I suppose it derives from the unconscious gesture of rolling one's eyes heavenward looking for the lost words or cue. My first memory is of being on my father's shoulders. We are looking up at a tall building. In a window near the top, I see my mother. She is waving. My brother has just been born, and my mother is in the hospital. I am three. To write this essay, to write anything, I search through my memories. I like to think of them, my memories, arranged in library fashion on ascending stacks of stacks. In my imagination, there is one of those open ladders, rollers at its top running in channels and wheels wearing grooves on the floor. The ladder glides along the shelving. What I need to remember has always been kept on the upmost spot, the hardest part to reach. A place has these hidden coordinates: time and memory. We *travel* there. Through time and within memory. We return to the time when . . . When we tour, we want our destinations to remain timeless or, at least, to remain stuck in the time we first experienced them. In Athens, at the Acropolis, literarily the Summit City, they are restoring the ruins of the Parthenon, deteriorating from the city's pollution, to a state of pristine ruin: the moment the temple was blown up in the nineteenth century. I grew up in Fort Wayne, Indiana, called the Summit City for its location along a long-gone canal system. When I go back, I experience that distortion of scale that comes with travel through time, with the animation of memory. Things grow smaller as you go up. Things grow smaller as you go back in time.

12

I walked up the Washington Monument, the stairs winding around the one central elevator shaft fenced off by a wire screen.

The occasional stone on the inside wall was inscribed by the donating charity, municipality, regiment. Here and there were scrubbed graffiti of the countless class trips. The windows on the cramped observation deck were miniscule, hard to get to as the current schoolchildren pressed in for a look. What I did see was the strange skyline of Washington, whose buildings are legislated to rise only so high as not to obscure the dome. It looked like about thirteen stories to me. An unlucky city, I thought. Off in the distance, I could glimpse the highrises of Virginia's Crystal City and the other taller obelisk dedicated to Washington by the Masons in Alexandria. The elevator delivered load after load of schoolchildren who rushed ten deep to the tiny windows. What had they come to see? What could they see? They were in a kind of space capsule not unlike the Apollo module that they had just seen at the Smithsonian. But now they were at the top of the rocket. A quick check out all the windows assured them of that. "Look!" they shouted. "Look how high up we are." And then it was time to go.

14

In the literature of elevators (Coover, Dahl, Whitehead), there is the moment when the car keeps going up. It is an extension of the initial wonder. Gravity has been resisted. The sky can now be scraped. The apparatus is so simple, so transparent, a parlor suspended by a thread. It is a daydream of elevator travel. The dream has you traveling in an elevator, pushing the button for the top floor, but as the vehicle arrives it rises above that, breaks through the ceiling, the roof, and keeps going on, up and up. As with all travel, it is the journey and not the destination. The protocol of elevator travel demands a silence among its occupants. No time here in the flight between floors for the dissertations of train travel, the memoirs of an ocean voyage, or even the interviews of the air. We become the center of gravity. We talk to ourselves. We dream our dreams. We contemplate claustrophobia, acceleration, even death. You have your excuse, this booth. For many it is a routine routine, a daily affirmation. This is a mechanized meditation. This is a special species of stillness at the heart of our teaming urban hives. We enter. We arrange ourselves. We face the closing doors. We suspend our animation. We go up.

Still Life of Sidelines with Bob

The Game Away from the Ball

Basketball coach Bob Knight of the Texas Tech University Red Raiders is riding the referee. It is the opening seconds of the home game with Oklahoma University, and the ref lucky enough to pull the assignment to patrol the bench-side corridor from Texas Tech's back court to Oklahoma's base line is weathering the sniping coming from Knight, pacing parallel. After a few minutes of this criticism, the ref has developed a twitch. He is flinching, his head turning toward the coach then shying away. Every call, no matter who is calling it, is being questioned, commented on, underscored. The ref's attention is being divided. His reaction time dulled. Running up the court, he stalls sooner after crossing the timeline, adding a bit more distance from the glowering coach. He is being conditioned. He can't take his eyes off his own periphery now. And then, like that, Coach Knight lays off, slumps into his chair and assumes the position, his arms wrapped around his broad chest, his head down, brooding, Olympian, his dark eyes looking out from beneath his dark and darkening brows, intent on the game before him.

I have no idea what is going on in the game. I have been forcing myself to watch this drama on the sidelines, one of Coach Knight's calculated contributions to the flow and tenor of the remaining minutes of play. Roger Angell has pointed out that in baseball, the only game where the ball doesn't do the scoring, the spectator must widen the field of vision to the whole playing field. Basketball fans certainly know of the game away from the ball—the screens and constant cuts, the choreography of checks and switches, pickups and block-outs performed covertly while the player in possession dribbles into position or coils in anticipation of the perfect bounce pass to the now-open man. In spite of sensing the complete action of the court, that bouncing ball more than likely rivets the fan's attention, its trajectory through the air mesmerizes. That is why I have had to expend so much energy to ignore the attractive nuisance of that ball in its flight and the furious action swirling around it to focus on the now-still center that is Coach Bob Knight.

In his thirty-five years of coaching college basketball, he has constantly shifted our attention to the game away from the ball. By that I don't mean simply the machinations of his players on the floor or even his psychological gamesmanship on the sidelines. It still matters that teams he coaches win, that the ball goes through his team's hoop more than the other team's. After thirty-five years in the presence of Bob Knight, however, the game away from the ball has expanded way beyond the game on the floor, in the arena, in the league, in the season. The game away from the ball has expanded to include institutions, state governments, whole peoples even. Our vision has shifted. We no longer keep our eye on the ball. Our eye is drawn to Knight.

Dazzleflage

Coach Knight, inert in his chair on the sidelines, wears a black pullover. Black is one half of Tech's colors. The other is scarlet, the shade of the collar of the golf shirt he has on beneath the black sweater.

There are a couple of things odd about this black. For one, it's not red, or more exactly, crimson, a color of Indiana University, where Coach Knight coached famously for twenty-nine seasons. The scarlet at his throat today is a tease, sharing some of the same frequency of that other red, but it is eclipsed by that expanse of smothering black. This black, the black of his sweater, is matte, flat, a color drained of color, and it could stand for all that will not be spoken about the history of his years in Indiana and his departure from the university where he was, until recently, so closely identified. The media guide I got along with my souvenir basketball scrupulously records his statistics of victory, the irresistible climb to 800 wins, the three national championships, the Olympic gold medal, the histories and careers of the scholar-athletes he nurtured during those years. It also scrupulously deletes the acrimony of his firing from IU, the legacy of controversy, the public displays of anger, the accusations of bullying, the actual acts of violence. There is, then, this absence. The black is a hole at the core of the excitement about the commencement of this new winning tradition at Tech.

The color of the sweater itself not what I want it to symbolize, its black does seem to absorb light, to flatten the figure who wears it. It is a kind of camouflage. It is a countershading that is goofing with my ability to read, in folds of cloth and the way light falls on fabric, the distance and depth of an object. The object I'm looking at, Coach Knight, is collapsing, collapsing in on himself. As I stare at him, from my perch on the mezzanine, he is beginning to, well, disappear.

It's funny I should be thinking of camouflage, as this is the game where students, on their own initiative, have created a new T-shirt on sale for the first time in the arena's Double T shop. Rising behind the bench and Coach Knight, the stands emit the traditional broad swatches of black-and-scarlet-clad boosters arrayed in bands of color into which the coach is beginning to blend. Here and there among the solid blocks of color are veins of these new camouflage shirts. The usual smattering of forest camo browns and greens, the woodland splotches and smears, have been replaced on these tees by shades of scarlet, white, pink, and black. The shirts' jumpy patterns disrupt the ironed-on message. "The General's Army," it says, invoking Coach Knight's nickname. As the game goes on, the camouflage pattern extends deeper into the crowd, marbling through the monochromatic black and red sections as more and more fans snap up the shirts and put them on.

There is another style of camouflage used in nature and war. Dazzle. Zebras, for instance, or referees for that matter, running in packs, are visually obvious to the predators that stalk them; they aren't blending into a background. But the high contrast of their striping creates another type of illusion, not blending, but that of an explosion right in front of our eyes, a scattering of the whole into many odd parts. For a while there at IU, Coach Knight had a liking for loud plaids and patterns of crimson and cream, the harlequin design of dazzleflage warships so obviously there in the sights of the submarine but so hard to get a bead on.

Bob Knight has always hidden himself in plain sight. His world-class temper could be either the real thing or a stunning act of diversion. The discipline he brings to bear on his players might be sadistic meanness or a calculated performance deployed to motivate and inspire. Or they could be both. They could be both real and a simulation of what is real. When he explodes, he could explode or simply seem to explode. It might depend on what we who are watching desire to see.

The Coach Knight I see on the bench is like a duplicate, a replica of the real Coach Knight. This Coach Knight, in the black sweater, is a quotation of the former red-sweatered Coach Knight. Getting down the sartorial look, the mane of silver hair, the beady stare, is relatively easy. It will be more difficult to duplicate the career at Indiana, its heights of success and its spectacular crashes. In a column introducing Coach Knight to Texas quoted in the media guide, Cynthia and Randy Farley liken him to one of Hemingway's heroes, but they neglect to connect both the coach and author to the danger of their powerful creations, the trap of self-parody. Playing one's larger-than-life self becomes a monumental task. Perhaps reconstituted in Texas, this Coach Knight's only remaining real disguise is a satire of a former self.

Pas de Deux with Chair

To advertise *A Season on the Brink*, ESPN's first made-for-television movie, the network features a reenactment of the moment during Indiana's game against Purdue in the '84–'85 season when Coach Knight launched a plastic bench chair on to the court while a Purdue player was shooting a technical foul shot. The verb is important. "Launched." "Threw." "Hurled." The coach in his new book, *Knight: A Coach's Life*, deploys "toss," transforming the verb into a noun to title the incident "The Chair Toss," and says only that he "sent it scooting" while devoting a mere page or so to it all. He professes he is baffled by the notoriety and the longevity of the scene. Its power, however, is undeniable.

It may have been the impetus for John Feinstein, author of *A Season on the Brink*, the book from which ESPN's movie is adapted, to approach Coach Knight in the first place for access to cover the '85–'86 season. Feinstein views it as the nadir of a Knight decline bracketing the previous year with the pinnacle of the summer's Olympic victory in Los Angeles. Coach Knight, the student of history, discounts the chair toss in comparison to the other sideline antics of other coaches. "I consider my link to infamy," he writes, "a pretty tame one." The critical turning point that afternoon represents to him has to do with what he was wearing. He writes that it had been the first time, in a fit of frustration, he had not worn a coat and tie for a game. Had he, he says now, the jacket would have been out on the floor, not the chair. Ever since then, however, he has worn those golf shirts and the sweaters.

Not only did ESPN feature the pas de deux with chair in the commercial, it was, in each commercial, repeated several times. There it goes again and again in a kind of action stutter, cut like the multiple renditions of tables tipped in a music video's cliché of rage or a Wild Bunch ballet of blood where the same wounded cowboys fall over and over to the ground. The image of the chair sailing out over the floor is indelible, and the gesture does seem inexhaustible in its ability to deliver a kind of aesthetic delight to its witnesses. Let's see that again!

Why should the legs on the graphic images of the event surprise Coach Knight? For him it was only an act. It was staged. The coach admits as much in his memoir when arguing its trivial nature by pointing out that no one was hit.

"I made sure," he writes, "it didn't come close to anyone." It looks, to everyone but the coach, like a spontaneous authentic eruption of extreme emotion, a kind of inarticulate expression of feeling, but we are told that it was, in fact, under control, scripted even, choreographed. He would have us believe that what we are seeing is theater, but what we believe we are actually seeing is real life.

Coach Knight is toeing a line here as delicately as he toed the sideline when he threw the chair. He didn't actually go himself out on to the floor. That would have been a real transgression. In order for theater to work its Aristotelian magic the audience must recognize that what they are seeing is within the context, the frame, of a theater. There, in the confines of art, we can exercise those emotions that if expressed outside of the theater in the real world would be truly dangerous. We watch in horror and pity as Oedipus blinds himself at the same time we know that the man before us acting as Oedipus has not really been blinded. Art is framed deviance. The artist doesn't simply create the picture but also creates the means for the audience to see it.

Bob Knight is, then, a kind of performance artist. And the various arenas, gyms, and field houses are the sites of the theater of Bob Knight. So often we can see the results of his art, the stunning residue of basketball genius performed within the painted lines that frame the varnished wood floors. But at other times we miss or he neglects to transmit the signal that he is performing. Often the frames he creates, if in fact he creates them, are less clear. There is a kind of slippage in the viewers' perception that results in the registering of real horror, not its simulated aesthetic twin.

Look, here is another piece of tape. Coach Knight throttling a player's neck. Here is another. A player head-butted by the coach on the bench during a time-out. And here is another. A scene before Assembly Hall in Bloomington, a student drawn up verbally and physically after exchanging a few words with the coach. In all these instances the frame Coach Knight asserts for these confrontations is that he was in the midst of a performance, a performance of instruction. What we are being asked to witness is a teacher, teaching. There's the frame. Can we see it that way? We are compelled to watch these moments over and over again to try to assess the shadowy context. This confusion itself is interesting. Is the actor out of control or is the actor acting out of control?

Not Oedipus as much as Hamlet here. Early in the play Hamlet tells us he will feign madness in order to attain his ends. Later Hamlet apologizes for his part in the deaths of Ophelia and her father. He reminds anyone who'll listen that he was mad.

There is drama on the basketball court but it is drama you can see because of the frame of "game." The chair, a light plastic floating shell of a chair, tossed onto the court that day shattered the illusion that it was a game. It was no longer play or a play.

Niceness and Nuts

In the seats behind Coach Knight on the bench are four men who have paid $750 a piece to sit there. One of them holds up a hand-lettered sign occasionally. From where I sit, it is hard to read, but I see the words "Hoosiers" and "Knight." Hoosiers for Knight perhaps. They have come from Indiana not only for the game but for proximity to the man. They've attended a practice and the Texas Tech training table and later, after the game, will sit by me at the news conference. They bid for their places today some months ago at a Tech fund raiser in Floyd's Knobs, Indiana, hosted by Coach Knight that, until recently, had raised money for Indiana University.

It is a weird coincidence that the United Spirit Arena in Lubbock is on Indiana Avenue, that it is made of bricks made in Indiana, that its inaugural game three years ago was won by a

Bob Knight–coached Indiana team. The landscape of Lubbock itself is like a Bizarro Indiana. It is flatter than the flattest part of my home state. Its surrounding farms seem more farmy, the fields measured in sections, not just acres. And the township grid, a signature of the quilted Indiana countryside, is even more pronounced here. Lubbock has out Indiana-ed Indiana.

Bob Knight, from Orrville, Ohio, spent twenty-nine years in Indiana, a state identified, if it has any identity at all, with the game of basketball. The ESPN movie features documentary interludes where real Hoosiers speak adoringly of their coach and their game. My mother reports from Fort Wayne that now the malls not only stock IU and Purdue licensed merchandise but Texas Tech stuff as well. Bob Knight's story has always been and continues to be a story also about Indiana.

Believe me, it is a burden being nice. When you inhabit The Heartland in this country, which this country also calls The Flyover, you begin to live this crazy contradiction. You believe, on the one hand, that you are the center of all that is good, true, and valuable. You are, you believe, the embodiment of American values and traditions, whatever they are. But simultaneously you know, in your heart of hearts, you are also in the middle of Nowheresville. So you keep up appearances. You're honest, optimistic, innocent, polite, respectful, and most of all nice. Nice is us. We are nice to the nth degree. And yet, it wears on you, keeping alive the flame of civility you believe is the flame of civilization.

In my favorite episode of *Law and Order*, a New York City woman who has murdered her sister to assume her identity is finally cornered by the DA. You took your sister's life, he accuses. And she answers, "My sister lived in Terre Haute, Indiana. She had no life."

Hoosiers, being nice, won't talk about this: Bob Knight is a monster. But he is our monster.

Because he won, because his program was clean, because his players graduated, because he played by the rules, especially because he played by the rules, because, finally, all of that was, well, nice, we allowed him to be something more. Because he was so very nice he could also become, for Hoosiers, the anti-Hoosier as well. He became for us, who constitutionally can't act out, our designated hitter, our surrogate rage against those stupid rules, our projection of the best-suppressed id on any forbidden planet. He is the thing in us all spoiling to be not nice.

You, who are Not Nice by nature, cannot begin to imagine how thrilling it is for the Nice to witness such public displays of emotion, any emotion, that Bob Knight could concoct. How the pent-up grudges, the slights, the nagging doubts, the inferiority, the martyrdom, the secret vanity, the righteousness even, and all those virtues that we must maintain and nurture, all of it gets bled off by the maniac in the bright red shirt. All heck, as we say, breaks loose.

I look at the four Hoosiers hovering behind Coach Knight. I wonder if the change of venue to this Bizarro Indiana will still work its empathetic catharsis. I can't imagine Texans plugging into this dynamic. Where is the understatement to foil the flamboyance? It's not quite the same. Bob Knight sits quietly on the Texas Tech bench. All around me Texans are going nuts as their team takes a commanding lead. But all the Hoosiers in the house wait on the Coach and on what he will do next.

My Father Has Been Turned into a Monstrous Vermin

My Father Turned into a Monstrous Vermin

I was in Fort Wayne for the millennium's New Year's celebration. My mother was on the municipal committee that had planned the year's events that culminated with the fireworks launched from the top of the Summit Bank Building downtown. Freezing, the crowd below watched the display from the new park built with the proceeds derived from another recent celebration, the bicentennial of the city's founding in 1774. The park was a wonderful legacy. It had been built on an often-flooded floodplain with a design that recognized that fact. The flowerbeds were planted with ornamental grasses, yellow flag iris, and bull rushes and reeds that thrived in swampy conditions. The fountains produced a fine primordial mist, subtly lit, that floated over the marshy fields. In the cold of that night, the misting fountains created a crystalline landscape both old and new as the citizens of Fort Wayne greeted the turning of the age.

My mother had been on the bicentennial committee as well, and, in both cases, she had been instrumental in the development of the mascots. The bicentennial wasn't hard to figure out. Someone dressed up as General Anthony Wayne and made the appearances at the parades, beer tents, plaque dedications, and battle reenactments. Johnny Appleseed was a close second—he's buried in Fort Wayne—but the general looked better in uniform and lacked the cooking pot on the head. And besides, General Wayne came equipped with a horse. The millennium required more brainstorming. My mother, always the poet, finally rested on the notion the millennium would best be represented by a millipede, a millipede she named, for no other reason than the alliterative, Millie.

A costume was commissioned. The millipede would be incredibly long. Most of it would be dragging along the ground. The segmented body suit in greenish velour and black velveteen piping had oversized antennae, bugged-out eyes, and a butterfly's coiled proboscis. The multiple pairs of legs, only two pairs of which would be operable, were connected together in order for all of them to simultaneously move, marionette fashion, as the operator walked along.

My mother volunteered my father to be the bug. I teased her when I called home about the symbolism of the committee's mascot being a verminous scavenger.

"They're herbivorous," she replied.

"But hard to make cuddly, I bet," I said.

And what about having my father, her husband, appear for a year as this creepy crawly thing.

"No one will know," she said.

I had recently moved south, below the bug line as we like to say, the climatic zone where the winter wasn't cold enough to kill off insects. Infesting our new house, we discovered moving in, was a hatch of millions of millipedes or what we found out were millipedes once the county extension agent duly identified them. I have grown somewhat familiar to the flying roaches and the grasshoppers as large as small cats.

"You'd be surprised," my mother said, "about how cuddly your father is, millipede or not."

"You might have at least called him Milton or Mick the Millipede."

My father was good-natured about it all, suited up and crossed genders. My mother sent pictures of Millie in the parades, at the ribbon cuttings, in front of the huge numbers counting down on the official digital clock. I received a video of the ceremony in the park, the burial of the time capsule. I saw my father as the giant creature wave his many hands at the camera, inch his way through the festive crowd with the gold-plated shovel. He looked like a bad special effect, a monster from a Japanese Godzilla film, his dragging tail cutting a swath of destruction through a twig and tissue paper city.

By the time I actually saw him in costume in person on New Year's Eve, my father's tail had worn dramatically thin from the continuous friction of his various civic duties. They had taken to wrapping the nether region up over one shoulder of the upright upper half. The result was a commingling of legs or, now more accurately, arms that seemed to emanate from the lime body at every angle. That night the committee had sponsored a carnival for children at the Fine Arts Center to help them stay awake for the fireworks at midnight. The building was lousy with screaming kids doing spin art, singing karaoke, and having their faces painted. My father, as Millie, moved through the crowds. The children were strangely calmed by the hulking figure, magnetically drawn to hold one of its many hands as it slithered along. It led a little parade over to the park, the children still attached. Millie seemed to undulate through the ground-hugging fogs the fountains produced, lugging its cargo of limpid limpets. It stopped and turned dramatically to face the sound of the first exploding bombs going off above the city.

We Didn't Speak of Reddy Kilowatt

My grandfather worked as a meter reader for the municipal electric utility, City Light and Power, until it was sold to the regional for-profit company, Indiana and Michigan, or I&M, in a deal he regarded as shady.

I&M had always had a presence in Fort Wayne. That company owned the electric interurbans that ran all over Indiana early in the century. I&M maintained the high-tension transmission lines that brought much of the electricity into the city to be sold by City Light. There was a billboard near I&M's building, shielding the lot where it kept the hulks of transformers, generators, and cable spools. The billboard was by the corner of Spy Run and State, and my grandfather had to read its meter. The sign, of course, was lit all the time, and sometimes parts of it moved. The billboard, advertising the advantages of electric power, utilized a character named Reddy Kilowatt—a stick figure made up of a skeleton of lightning with a light bulb head and a light bulb nose and socket outlets for ears.

My grandfather despised Reddy Kilowatt, and we weren't to speak of him. Not that we would have even noticed its existence without the focus of my grandfather's rage. Reddy Kilowatt would have been just another cartoon on the landscape of cartoons I wandered through as a child. Still, we knew the days Grandfather read the meter on the sign. He would come home restless and unsettled, drink an extra Pepsi on the back porch to facilitate his belching.

After City Light was bought out and he retired, my grandfather took elaborate routes through the city to avoid passing the sign. This was a difficult thing to do since State was the main east-to-west thoroughfare on the north side of town. There were times that passing the sign was unavoidable and the traffic light at the corner of Spy Run and State always stopped you. Grandfather seethed in the car as Reddy Kilowatt, his crimped kinetic arm waving back and forth, loomed before him.

Stopped at the same light on our journey across town to visit my grandparents, my family contemplated Reddy Kilowatt, who might then be wearing earmuffs for winter or sunglasses during the summer, promoting electric heat or air conditioning. My mother always mentioned, her father not being present to hear, how Daddy was looking more and more like that Reddy Kilowatt—the wiry frame, the round mostly bald head with the tiny white shock of hair at his crown. "Don't tell him I said so, please!" she said as the light changed.

Hoosier Defines Itself

My uncle went to graduate school at Tennessee to study health. He got a government grant to run a study in the hope of demonstrating the validity of his thesis: To know the deleterious effects of obesity would aid in weight reduction. He had two groups of dieters. The control group simply followed the menus and exercise suggestions provided by a national weight reduction company. The subjects in the experiment also had to follow the diet and in addition complete a rigorous course detailing graphically and statistically the dangers of fat. To his surprise, my uncle proved that while the control group modestly lost pounds, the educated group effortlessly gained a ton. Traumatized by the detailed information they were receiving, they nervously ate in order not to think about what was happening to their bodies as they ate.

While in Knoxville, my uncle sent me a poster I hung on the wall of my bedroom. The drawing depicted a team portrait of the mascots of the Southeastern Conference, their eponymous heads bobbing above the various team football uniforms. There were two Bulldogs, a Hog, and several military combatants— Mississippi's Rebel, Vanderbilt's Commodore, and Tennessee's own Volunteer. Alabama's Tide was, strangely, an Elephant that would make no sense until, years later, I moved to Tuscaloosa and learned it derived from the historical confluence of a Rose Bowl game and a local luggage company. Right after my uncle's gift, my father gave me the complementary poster representing the Big Ten, and I taped it next to the first one. I liked to think of the two portraits as my uncle's two groups of dieters.

The head of the Hoosier was rendered as that of a bumpkin, the dictionary definition after all, the same definition that Dan Quayle once on the floor of the United States Senate argued to legally change. The Hoosier on the poster showed up as a yokel, a rural rube with a fraying straw hat atop his rusty head of hair. He had vacant blue eyes and freckles, big lips and buckteeth that gnawed on a bent straw of a wheat stalk or weed stem. This Hoosier, even wearing a big-shouldered football uniform, not the requisite blue denim bib overalls, didn't look very competitive surrounded by the vicious menagerie of Wildcat, Badger, and Wolverine.

There is a whole class of mascots that suffer in this modern era of corporate corporeal identity. Look at the Buckeye looking like an eyeball with eyes. Adjectives get attached. Hurryin' was wed to Hoosier. Or weapons are issued, a pitchfork, say, that arms the Hoosier as an animated American Gothic. For a while there, the Indiana mascot metamorphed into a bison. I believe it derived from the state's seal, in which a pioneer with an axe fells a tree while the silhouette of a bison lights out for the territories. In the end Hoosier is just what it is. It is the word itself, its own mascot. One year, perhaps the same year native son Quayle rose in the Senate, the state tried to change the motto on the license tags from Hoosier State to Heritage State and was met with near insurrection. No one really knows what a Hoosier is, but not knowing, as my uncle proved, has its own logic. A Hoosier is a Hoosier is a Hoosier.

The State Drink of Wisconsin

The state bird of Wisconsin is the robin. The state flower of Wisconsin is the wood violet. The state tree of Wisconsin is the sugar maple. The state animal of Wisconsin is the badger. The state wild animal of Wisconsin is the white-tailed deer. The state domesticated animal of Wisconsin is the dairy cow and the various breeds—Holstein, Brown Swiss, Guernsey, Jersey, etc.—take yearly turns. The state fish of Wisconsin is the muskellunge. The state insect of Wisconsin is the honeybee. The state mineral of Wisconsin is galena. The state rock of Wisconsin is red granite. The state soil of Wisconsin is antigo silt loam. The state symbol of peace of Wisconsin is the mourning dove. The state of Wisconsin is undecided on the state of Wisconsin's drink. The legislature continues to argue the issue. Beer could be the state drink of Wisconsin. Milk could be the state drink of Wisconsin. Or both beer and milk.

Touchdown Jesus

My father liked to take me to football games at Notre Dame. He liked to point out how gold the gold on the helmets of The Fighting Irish was, how they were as gold as the gold on the dome of the big building on the campus we could see from the stadium. Navy's helmets were gold and Pitt's helmets were gold but not as gold as Notre Dame's gold helmets. I saw O. J. Simpson play in South Bend. We always sat in the end zone, and I remember watching him hauling in the kickoff ball and starting his sprint up the field right before us. I saw Roger Staubach and Navy in a snowstorm. Crushed tight together in the stands, everyone wore heavy wool coats before the coming of down parkas and Gore-Tex. I was there when Dan Devine's team changed its uniform to the green jerseys from the blue. The entire stadium went crazy seeing this brand new team emerge from the tunnel. And I remember when Notre Dame built the library beyond the other end of the stadium and finished off the nine-story facade with a mosaic of a beatific Christ, His arms raised above His head, in the jubilant gesture of the referee signaling a score. He hovered, it seemed, above the goal posts, above the thronging crowd, above the teeming stadium, the Goodyear blimp drifting above His head, exhorting us all. Touchdown! Touchdown! Touchdown!

We always got there early. Sometimes we stayed by the car and tailgated in the parking lot, eating our lunch from a cooler in the trunk. But more often, especially when we were with some of my father's old high-school teammates, we would all drift over to the field house to look at the names of the lettermen on sacred plaques, admire the immaculate cases of memorabilia, trophies, and photographs of the old great and holy teams. My father had gone to Central Catholic in Fort Wayne. They had been the Fighting Irish too, and in his senior year, his team had won the mythical state football championship. My father, who had been quarterback, and his old backfield would recite the names on the plaques, remind each other of games they'd played in or seen.

Most of all I liked it when we went to the far end of the stadium before the game, to the locker room door. A crowd had always gathered to wait and watch for the Notre Dame players to emerge alone or in small groups, threes or fours, from their campus dorms and drift toward the stadium, wading through the crowd into the locker room. The players were huge. None of them had necks. They were stuffed into the insignia-dripping letter jackets of dark blue wool with glossy blue-black leather sleeves.

Touchdown Jesus looked down on us all gathered in the plaza before the locker room door. Look, there were some more coming our way! Often, just by the door, there was a boy—it was never the same boy—about my age, waiting in his wheelchair or leaning on his crutches, his body mangled into a cast or contorted or quaking with palsy. The players had been tipped to his presence. The crowd parted as they approached. The players tolerated the back-pats and the praise as we moved to make room. We just wanted to touch them, to get a word in. They said "excuse me" politely, didn't stop for us as they made their irresistible journey toward the door. But when they spotted the kid by the door they were drawn to him and to the football that miraculously appeared in the folds of his hospital blankets, in the crook of his traction-set arm. We all watched as each player took the ball to sign it, signed it, and handed it back to the bandaged kid, saying a few inaudible—to us—words and then tousling his hair with their beefy hands before disappearing into the changing rooms to be transformed for the game.

My Mother Invents a Tradition

At our dining room table in the house on Clover Lane in Fort Wayne, my mother made it all up. She was the dean of girls at Central High School. The city school system had announced Central's closing and the busing of its students to the six other high schools in the system, two of them, Northrup and Wayne, just being built. Mom would be going to Northrup, and her job now was to manufacture the particulars of the new school's identity. There was a committee, a group of students and teachers drawn from the constituencies of Central and the two northside schools siphoned off by the expansion.

I remember the group listening to records of marching bands

playing fight songs and alma maters, the words absent, in our living room. They rated the melodies on graph paper with scales from 1 to 10. "This is 'On Wisconsin!'" my mother would say. And one evening the band uniforms and cheerleading costumes were modeled and judged there too, but that was much later. My mother had to do the heavy lifting of the task force, actually writing the words to the songs the band members would play in the future. She would also narrow down all the choices of styles and colors in the catalogues she gathered from the wholesalers of academic garb, the purveyors of embroidery and emblems, the flag-makers, the jewelers, trophy stores, yearbook printers, decal suppliers, and fund-raising companies. Then she would guide the committee to her favorites.

At the dining room table she had to get herself in the mood for her creations. For this new school she was constructing a nostalgic past out of nothing. It was named for a former super-intendent, no help there. So she relied on the stored memories of her own high school, the images of high school created in mov-ies she saw while she was in high school. There had been ivy on the red brick walls and a senior door only seniors could walk through. Every year the graduating class planted a climbing rose bush along the fences of the stadium, and the trowel used for the job was handed down to the next class at a ceremony in the spring as the roses budded and began to bloom. Northrup had none of these rituals as of yet, it was being built in a scraped-flat cornfield on the northern edge of town. The excavation left a few trees from a woodlot nearby, and mother mused to me that perhaps that could become a lover's lane. She imagined the moon over the copse of trees. "The students," she wrote for the students in the new handbook, "call this spot Lover's Lane."

I was in high school then, at North Side, my mother's high school, the one she waxed with nostalgia as she worked at the dining room table. At North Side now no one remembered why the seniors gave a garden trowel to the junior class. The rose bushes had been torn out during a renovation before I started there.

She went with orange and brown for Northrup's colors, presented them to the committee as a fait accompli. It was the early '70s, and those colors were hot. Our sofa was orange and brown striped. The other new high school, Fort Wayne Wayne—I know, it is very funny name—was forced into red, white, and blue since its mascot, the General, followed from the name. Mom had more leeway and went with the palette of the moment. She trusted that her words for the school songs, the cheers, the student codes, and the orientation materials would give the colors a patina, age them in a tea of her own emotional past.

The mascot would be a Bruin. This seemed more sophisticated than the simple Bear, and perhaps it fit the same logic of euphemism left over from Central, the school that was closing, where the team mascot, Tiger, had also been known as the Bengals in the sports pages. Bruin went nicely with the earthy tonic expressed in the newly selected colors, rhymed with ruin, and suggested the whole conceit for student publications. The newspaper, she decided, would be called *What's Bruin* and the yearbook known for years to come as *Bear Tracks*.

At the dining room table she wrote the poems that became the fight song and the alma mater. I have no notion of the words themselves. They survive to this day, sung at assemblies and home games. I went to a different school and never had to learn them. I can remember her singing, though, trying to fit her words into the scansion of the appropriated songs. As I watched her sing a few bars then stop and erase then sing a few notes more, I was making this memory of my mother creating memories and the myths of memory. A few scraps of cloth. A totem or two. Some new arrangement of the same old words hooked to a persistent jingle.

A Cyclone of Cardinals

Midwesterners like to think a tornado is the region's official natural phenomenon. It's their pet weather, their special storm. The twister in the black and white Kansas of the movie is more powerful and magical than anything in glitzy Oz. The citizens of Xenia, Ohio, where all the tornado alleys empty, speak nervously but with a kind of pride about their repeated visits of destructions. With its precision and its paradoxes, a tornado fits organically into the landscape of open plains and cleared spaces where its victims can see the funnels dancing on the horizon, chase them across the checkerboard of the farm fields and feedlots.

I lived for a while in Ames, Iowa, where Iowa State University adopted the Cyclone as its mascot, the V of the vortex twirling on the sides of football helmets, stationery letterhead, sweatshirts, and baseball caps. But in Ames, for some reason, those graphic depictions were eclipsed by an icon of an angry cardinal. The designers had worked hard to make the bird look angry. Its beak curved into a permanent snarl. Its black eyebrow crooked above its glaring, staring eye. They had named the cardinal Cy, the name the umbilical back to the official atmospheric logo, I guess. It was, when I arrived, a mystery to me. Cartoon cardinals were everywhere, adorning outdoor advertisements, adhering to side panels of cars and trucks, decorating the facades of buildings where the more placid and real pigeons roosted in the flexed fiery combs on the heads of the giant representations. I gathered that any animal species made more sense to those people who orchestrate motivation. A bird, any bird, was more inspiring to rally around than a mere organized wind. Maybe. Maybe it was only symmetry that propelled the choice—the cardinal a kind of mirror image, an avian match for the cross-state rival Iowa's golden hawk schematic that stood for the Hawkeyes, whatever a Hawkeye was.

I discovered that Ames was an outlet for Collegiate Pacific, a company that manufactures licensed trademark apparel. I discovered this when I was taken to one of the factory's open houses where we locals were invited semiannually to come in and take the mistakes and misprinted items off their hands for a significantly reduced price. And that had been another thing I noticed about my new town. While the official cardinal had been the predominant mascot fauna, I couldn't help but notice the eclectic nature exhibited by the populace on their casual wear. Lions, tigers, bears. All manner of birds. Spartans, gladiators, Trojans. Fighting thises and thats. Pirates, cowboys, devils—blue, red, and green. Indians, chiefs, redskins, warriors, braves. Tarheels, Yankees, Rebels, Hoosiers, Buckeyes, Hawkeyes. Bulls, Browns, Bees. You name it. It was a kind of United Nations of proprietary images teaming with team identity.

On closer inspection you noticed the flaws at the sales and on the street—the ghost images of the double exposure, the smear of a misaligned silk-screen registration, the misspelled words, the missing letters. I loved the mad juxtapositions of multiple printings that created hybrids of logos and language—"University of University" or "ate State." Here on someone's back was, what? Here were the Jabberwocks—a swirling cloud composite of swords, lightning, and horses' hooves. Someone else displayed the Chimeras—a bestiary of eyes and beaks and the 4-H cloverleaf.

At the outlet sales the whole town rummaged through the mountains of rejects. Short- and long-sleeved T-shirts, sweatshirts with hoods and without, pullover sweatshirts, sweatshirts that zipped and those printed fleece-lined inside facing out, ponchos, sweaters, cardigans, windbreakers, blankets, towels, hats, caps, scarves, even the old felt pennants on a stick. I liked the rubbery feel of the paint on the cloth and all the Latin of the upside-down printed school seals. The open books, the oil lamps, the olive branches, the oak leaves and acorns, the palm fronds, the bells, the crosses, the earth, the moon, the planets, the stars.

It turned out that Collegiate Pacific also made a line of outfits for mascots, the kind with the foam rubber body suits and giant heads. I was told they had had a surplus cardinal suit lying around. Maybe the school that ordered it failed to take delivery, or they came up short with the payments and the company repossessed the bird, donating it to the hometown team. Besides, the architecture of a comparable Cyclone suit seemed impossible to construct with the available technology. Where would you put the eyes? Should a Cyclone even have eyes? It would keep coming out as an odd-looking cloud—dirty gray, nebulous, amorphous, simply wrong.

Then You Hit the Archer Over the Head with Your Ukulele

I wouldn't do it. I wouldn't take part in the rally's skit my mother had written and choreographed. I was five and in the habit of accompanying my mother downtown where she taught freshman English at Central High School. I had my own desk at the back of her classroom where I drew pictures of the Trojan War and Odysseus sailing home, the books she was teaching. She was also the faculty advisor for the booster club and I helped her sell candy, popcorn, and pop in the concession stands during the games. She spray-painted the spirit posters too, the message emerging in the burst of paint as she pulled away the masking letters. It also fell to her to run the weekly pep sessions. During basketball season they were in the tiny gym. I sat up by the drummers in the band, who taught me Central's signature rhythm, a backbeat syncopation that made the marchers skip on every fourth step. I liked to watch the Tiger on the floor, acting in my mother's morality plays. The Tiger suit consisted of the furry orange-and-black-striped footed pajama that zipped up the belly and a papier-mâché head I had helped my mother repair and paint. The head was very large. I could fit completely inside it curled up. It was hard to breathe wearing it, so the student inside would lift the head like a knight's visor to gulp in some air between cheers.

South Side, Central's archrivals, were the Archers, represented by a green leotarded Robin Hood. The Archer, in elf shoes, patrolled the sidelines with a long bow and a quiver of arrows. My mother had written me into her latest creation vanquishing the Archer. In it there were vignettes representing the history of the rivalry. I was supposed to be in the scene from the '20s. Dressed in kneesocks and knickers, raccoon-skin coat, and felt pork pie hat, I was to hit the Archer, who had tied up the Tiger with his own tail, over the head with my ukulele, freeing Central's mascot. Later in the sketch, all the historic characters did the Twist, then wildly popular, around the supine green body of the defeated foe.

For some reason I can't begin to remember I didn't want to do it. I do remember my mother and her students pleading with me during the rehearsal, telling me how cute I was and would be. It was hot in that coat. The Tiger had his Tiger head off completely. It wasn't that I was shy or I didn't know how to do the Twist. I understood the concept of the piece. I didn't have any lines to memorize. Perhaps I felt too responsible. What if I performed and the magic charm of that performance failed to work, the strings of my enchanted ukulele no match for the strung taut bow of the green archrival?

It had been just that fall my parents had taken me to Ball State, where my uncle was a student, to see the grand homecoming parade. Suddenly one of the Roman slaves, a fraternity pledge drafted to haul his house's float, broke free of his chains and ran right to me in the crowd. "You must save me," he cried, "Save me, please!" until his brothers, dressed as Legionnaires, dragged him back to the float. I must have been thinking of that incident months later in the Central gym. All these costumed people begging me to help, urged me to save the Tiger who stood there patiently, headless, happy to have this moment to catch his breath.

The War Dances of Redskins

I was a Redskin. I was a Redskin for three years when I attended North Side High School in Fort Wayne. Before that, in junior high, I had been a Chief. This was in Indiana, of course, a state named to honor, with the inaccurate name of Indian, the people killed, expelled, or assimilated in order to create a state named Indiana. The Miami mainly. Little Turtle's grave is just down the river from where my high school sits. The excavation there uncovered the remains of the sword presented to the chief by George Washington, etc. It was another excavation, however, the one on the sandy riverbank to lay the foundation for

North Side in 1926, that suggested the future name of its mascot. That dig uncovered an ancient midden, relics of teeth and bone, worked stone, a few beads, remnants of fire, maybe even a grave or two, and led to the honorific of "Redskin" attaching to the athletic teams of the new high school built on top of the site. The evidence of that excavation, its meager catalogue of artifacts, a residue of an indigenous pre-Columbian, perhaps, inhabitation, is today used as justification by those who want to retain "Redskin" as the mascot in the face of the occasional efforts to change it. See, the supporters say, there is a reason, a history, a tradition for the appellation. They miss the point, of course, of using this particular epithet, its particular nuance of that history and tradition. But never mind.

The name came with a character, a student in costume who danced before the start of football and basketball games. The costume was buckskin chaps and shirt with the leather fringe on the sleeves, a beaded breastplate and full-feathered headdress, more a plains get-up than the more accurate woodland outfit. But then what did we know. And the dance and the music that accompanied the costumed character were all Hollywood too. It was supposed to be a war dance, we imagined, with a lot of rhythmic bowing, hands outstretched, moving with a step that was both shuffle and skip in the inscribed outline of the tip-off circle. There might have been a hatchet or a lance.

A kid named Kevin was the best of the three students (there was a yearly competition) who held the position during the time I went to school. All arms and legs, Kevin added a twirling dervish turn to the movements, took his shirt off even during the late football season, danced around the lance (yes, there was a lance) he ceremoniously thrust into the ground. There was war paint too, on his face, red and white, the school colors, grease-based makeup streaked under each eye. The war paint had been applied over an initial coat of copper color he sponged onto all his exposed very white and freckly skin. Often the finish was splotchy, dappled.

Kevin didn't have enough time to get into makeup during the big riot. This was my junior year, the year the school system closed Central High School downtown, where my mother had taught English and been the dean of girls for nearly twenty years, and bussed its mostly black students out to the six white high schools around the city's edge. This was in the early '70s. The integration hadn't gone well, with every high school experiencing protests, beatings, fights, vandalism, and bomb threats. This was even true at the two new high schools, Wayne and Northrup.

At North Side the alienated black students staged a boycott of classes, and a schoolwide assembly was called by the fretting principal hoping to talk things out. We met in the gym. The football team and the cheerleaders were there, already clustered on the court with the frazzled administrators and coaches. The teachers patrolled the stands. Those squads on the floor had a semblance of harmony and order, having had to work together through practices in the summer. Kevin burst in, running half-dressed in his outfit, feathers flying, to his spot in the center of the floor. He was very white, I remember, without his makeup. He seemed to glow, reflecting the bright light of the new mercury vapor lamps just then reaching the peak of their illumination, having been turned on in haste as the crowds of students poured into the gym from all around the building. They shoved a microphone into his hands urging him to speak, and I remember thinking this breaks some unspoken code to which mascots adhere. The mute mascots were to remain silent on the sidelines as if they had appeared in our midst from some preverbal land where only pantomime, pep, and pumping fists were allowed. They are to always be illustrative in their stoic silence. Indians even more so.

But our Indian said something. Did he say to the throng of angry and frightened students packed into the bleachers that we were all Redskins? Did he say it? "We are all Redskins!" I hope he said it. And then he did the dance. Yes, he did the dance. A skeletal band had been mustered, the drums beating the tom-tom and a trumpet blaring that warning staccato. We watched Kevin dance the dance.

I don't remember what happened then, but we all ended up dancing on the gym floor. Marvin Gaye was on the speakers. The Stones. Carole King. We were studying *Tapestry* in Mrs. Neuhaus's English class.

The cheerleaders reminded us to take off our shoes before we ventured out on the gym floor. We filled that floor. We were on the edge of a riot, on the verge of a party. The administrators began to look relieved. We didn't talk. What could we say? Dancing seemed like the thing to do at the time. We were so many, nearly two thousand, we couldn't do much more than mill in time to the music that didn't stop, it seemed, for hours. We danced that way, in a kind of trance, until the buses came.

The Mother's March

I went with my mother when she went door-to-door in the neighborhood, collecting for the March of Dimes. She let me push the doorbells. I liked the illuminated ones that blinked out when I depressed them. Mother and I would visit with many of the neighbors who invited us in for a chat and for something to warm us up. This was after the polio vaccines. We had all just taken the sugar cube the summer before. The charity had altered the focus of its appeal to birth defects, but most often my mother and our neighbors shared memories of polio—the closing of the river beach, the braces and the iron lungs, Roosevelt. I drank hot chocolate and sometimes got to play at playing someone's piano. At home, my mother would let me separate the big pile of coins we collected into smaller piles of pennies, dimes, nickels, and quarters.

"The first thing I did when I saw you for the first time was count your fingers and toes." She had been knocked out completely for my birth. I had been delivered with forceps. I picture her groggily counting my fingers and toes. They're all there.

Years later, I came to realize that during those treks through the neighborhood my mother regarded me as a kind of mascot. I was an emblem of her luck as a mother, both the charm that embodied the wish and the body itself charmed into existence. I was illustrative of the charity's objectives. See, all his fingers tickling the keys of your piano, depressing the buttons of your doorbells. I was no cartoon, no stylized rendering of the talisman, not even a poster child. I was just her son, but that was enough for metaphor.

Ephemera

Two Postcards

I have two picture postcards I picked up in Hannibal, Missouri. One has two boys equipped, as you'd suspect—Tom and Huck. Straw hats, bib overalls rolled at the cuff, bare feet. Backs to us, they are watching a steamboat, of course, cruise by on the Mississippi. Illinois, the card's caption says, is in the background. The other card shows the stern-wheeler *Delta Queen*, the last authentic steamboat, as it plies the same river. The view is from Riverview Park, Inspiration Point. They are old cards, maybe forty years old, published by the Becky Thatcher Gift Shop and printed in the USA. I got them in a bank that had been converted to a bookstore. The vault had been given over exclusively to the works of Mark Twain. The bookstore owner, a retired banker himself, swore the Huck of the postcard was his father. Hannibal is a strange town, stuck, as it were, in time. Stranger still since the time in which it is stuck is a fictional one. There are other such strange places like this—Green Gables, Sunnybrook Farm, Chincoteague Island—that have started out as actual places only to become fictional places and then became, well, real ones once again. Readers who journeyed to them in their reading now visit for real. The time of the fiction must be maintained within the present time. Life becomes a kind of perpetual permanent pageant. Hannibal also maintains an additional petrified, parallel time. Along with the reeenactors of Twain's books there are reenactments of Twain's last visit to his hometown a century ago. Then, he watched the fence being whitewashed by children recreating the children he created. Today you can see the same fence, the same whitewash, and children dressed the same way as they work. But also you see a "Mark Twain," a facsimile of Mark Twain, watch with you, see what you see.

General Delivery

Letters are from another time. I don't simply mean that any letter as an artifact preserved from the time of its making is from another time. Or that these letters written a century ago by Mark Twain and "S. L. Clemens" survive into our own present. I was thinking of the Letter itself, the technologies of its manufacture and distribution. Letters are like those stern-wheeled steamboats, floating museums, and almost as rare these days. Post offices retain that ancient feel as well despite their immersion in the systems of computers, scanners, and automated sorters. I ask that my postcards be hand-cancelled, the time and place of the actual transaction affixed by an antique rubber stamp and ink, the two-step thump of pad strike then stamp stomp. The Letter is handcrafted, hand-handled, hand-delivered. The PO, then, is a portal back to this past, a post of the past, a node of the analog embedded within the instant transmissions of the age. I am thinking of the Post Office, not the post–Post Office of the present Postal Service. When I vacation in Maine, I send my hand-cancelled postcards abroad with the request that my correspondents reply via General Delivery, attaching the addresses of nearby POs. During my stay, I return daily to the windows at Stonington, Deer Isle, Little Deer Isle, Sunrise, etc., and ask if there's any mail for me. And I love that the clerk is not surprised I am asking, asks my name, and turns to the pigeonhole that might contain the possibility. Wherever I go, I ask for the mail. You never know. I never know. Something might be waiting there with my name on it.

Counting Words

In his letter titled "A Private Word," Mark Twain informs his correspondent that he has "spilt 48,000 words in 34 days" during his stay in York, Maine. A century later, words don't count and aren't counted in exactly the same way. I haven't seen a photocopy of the actual letter. Is it a holograph? I am reading a typescript from a print taken from an e-mail. Was it typed? Twain invested in the gadget, right? He was one of the first "writers" to type. I like to think of several machines in cases among the trunks lugged to that beach. It would have made the counting easier, standardizing the line length and the number of lines per page, making it a snap, then, to average and add. It is strange when you think about it—that the business of writing would be settled then by such piecework. Paid by the word! How styles might have been even more deflected if the wage scale was by the letter, a wholly different kind of padding. It is much more rare today to be paid by the word. The piecework has been exchanged for the negotiated price of a finished product. You can see Twain counting up the coin at the end of the day, satisfying a need, perhaps, to demonstrate that a concrete thing was under construction. The typewriter answers that nineteenth-century need perfectly—like repeating rifles, sewing machines, harvesters, machines that build other machines. With a typewriter you could get some production going. Twain would have loved this machine, the one I am using right now. Right below this line, in the borders of the opened window every word I type is duly counted. There are two numbers actually, pulsing and flashing, one representing the total number of words typed and the other the number of the word closest to the blinking cursor. This word—*word*—for example, is word #919, a mere pittance compared to the summer's production noted by Twain. The irony is that it is so much more efficient now to count but that the words don't count in the same way anymore. Another irony is that I have set up this incredible typesetting machine to replicate the look and feel of the nineteenth-century typewriter. The font, the margin settings, the leading—all mimic a product of the century before. I even have a font that counterfeits the varying pressure of various key strikes—the *a* lightly struck by the left pinky finger, the lasso of the *e* filled in by what appears to be a heavy residue of ribbon ink. Of course these letters we are looking at are copies anyway, the originals sent and perhaps lost long ago. Carbon paper, another blast from the past, has been reduced to a fossil of the *cc* in the e-mail address field. The editor of this magazine has asked for 1,000 to 1,200 words on these 250 (give or take) words written by Mark Twain. This is word #1105.

Lots

When he died, Nick Karanovich had the largest private collection of Twain ephemera in the world. He was a middle-school principal in my hometown, Fort Wayne, Indiana. At auction the collection garnered the estate $1.4 million, and a dealer from Texas carted off the remaining unsold material in three North American moving vans. I visited Nick's house once. From the outside it looked like all the other houses in the suburban track development—a split-level with an attached two-car garage. The garage wasn't a garage. It was the fireproof vault where he stored the paper. It all started when he stumbled upon a first edition of *The Adventures of Tom Sawyer* at an estate sale. The room, the garage that was not a garage, was windowless and the temperature and humidity were controlled. There was hardly room to walk amid the boxes and files and cases stuffed with papers and books. Just a narrow pathway from the door to a wooden desk in the room's center, a desk with an authentic provenance as a launching pad for so many Mark Twain missives. I sat where the writer sat in a chair where he purportedly sat, or I almost did since I was really sitting deep inside a specially constructed bunker that simulated the experience by bringing together this desk and chair. It was another machine, that room. It too trafficked in time travel. Nick had constructed it to operated like a nuclear pile, hoping to accumulate some critical mass of Twainia. But it was all already decaying, doing the half-life two-step in the other direction. I love the fact that the other letter found in Maine, a letter never known nor possessed by Nick Karanovich, seems to be about returning something, a razor, and an exchange of money. Long ago that message was set in motion. Now these little pieces of time have been found and are circulating again, a paradox of entropy as well as its proof.

Country Roads Lined with Running Fences

A DOZEN STORY PROBLEMS ABOUT THE PLACE OF PLACE

1. Where to have lunch? One summer, in Centerville, Iowa, I had supper in a restaurant on the largest town square in the world. At one time, chances were good that on most town squares of the Midwest there would be a steak place, or a pizza parlor, soda fountain, or newsstand, run by a Greek family. Perhaps the only indication would be a special salad on the menu, a gyros machine by the grill, or a fading picture of a white island and blue water tacked to the wall. Ten years before, George, the restaurant owner, came to Centerville from the Peloponnese by way of the Quad Cities, where he had family in the restaurant business. He worked most of the year but shut down to return to Greece with his family. He told me he sent his wife and child back for good since he wanted the boy to grow up there. One day, he thought, he'll return for good, too. It was the winter he had never grown used to. Though Centerville had been very good for business, it could never be home. When I told him how much I'd liked traveling in Greece, how I'd look to make it over there again, he did something remarkable. He scribbled down his name and the addresses of cousins in Athens, folks in his village, and told me where to find them when I am in Kalamata. "Ask for Yiorgos," he said. "Say that you are from Iowa."

2. *Iowa is where exactly?* Actually, I am from Indiana—that's where I was born and grew up. I know the feel of the Midwest. In Ireland, in Poland, in Italy one can sense a loss and a resignation to the fact that much of the country's population lives somewhere else. America as a nation has never suffered a diaspora, but natives of Iowa, of Indiana, and of the Midwest know of this fate. Our migrations are internal, our shifts of population covered by an easy freedom to move about and an illusion that most places are the same or can be made to feel the same. Talking with George in Centerville, Iowa, reminded me of Greece, where most everyone has a friend or relative who has gone away. And being reminded of that brought me home, back to Iowa, to Indiana, to my midwestern home, where people have not gone to a new country but have certainly gone away.

3. *Where exactly is this Midwest?* Where are its borders? What are its colors on the map? It depends on whom you ask. Iowans generally sketch roughly the Big Eight states—Iowa, Nebraska, Kansas, Missouri, and the Dakotas—as the prime midwestern states. Sometimes they will reach for Oklahoma. When asked about Indiana or Ohio the usual consensus is that those places lie in the East. They are surprised to learn that Hoosiers think of the Midwest as the Big Ten—Michigan, Ohio, Indiana, Illinois, Wisconsin, and part of Iowa. Iowans want to know what "Easterners" from Indiana would call what they call the Midwest. I say the Plains, of course. It becomes more interesting when I ask what defines a midwestern state. It must be rooted in agriculture, they say. I answer that it should be a balance between farming and manufacturing. They narrow their definition. The agriculture must be a special kind. It must be corn. Their definition of the Midwest derives from their home state, of course. It hasn't defined anything at all, but has been shaped to fit the place.

4. Where exactly is the Midwest? We should perhaps be more interested in what the confusion reveals than in pinning down the actual boundaries of the place, though it is probably wise to spend a few moments in definition. Again, where is the Midwest? And beyond that, what does characterize the region? How does it differ from other regions? Does it differ at all? These are important questions in developing a sense of place. Perhaps we assign an identity too easily, use the names without thinking what we want them to represent. Despite the confusion about its location, people agree that the Midwest is a good place to be *from*. It is as if we keep the region purposely vague in order to include as many people as possible as natives. "I am *from* the Midwest": that coin is worth collecting.

5. What is the real question? So the real question is: Why do so many of us want to be from a place that is nowhere and everywhere? The preposition is important, the *from*. Even those of us who still live in the Midwest, no matter how you define it, still would say we are from the Midwest, as if its special properties rub off on us only at birth and that since birth we have been getting farther and farther away.

6. What is what it is not? Dorothy realizes when she bumps down in Oz that she is not in Kansas anymore. If there is anything that characterizes a literature of the Midwest, it is this sense of discovery through absence. Nick Carraway, the narrator of F. Scott Fitzgerald's *The Great Gatsby*, realizes as the story ends that it is a tale of the Midwest and of a midwesterner in New York totally unequipped to live in the East. As the novel ends, he is preparing to return home. Leaving home, the Midwest, in order to see home clearly is a driving force in the themes of midwestern literature and life. Stories of the Midwest often begin at the moment of turning back from afar and the hero gaining sight for the first time of a distant beauty. Living in the Midwest, we know a truth about this coming and going. Many, many people have left, but few actually return. Though Dorothy keeps demanding to be sent home, though she tells us once she is home that there is nothing like it, we are uneasy. It is a black and white world in Kansas. Why would she, why would we leave the technicolor of Oz?

7. What does New Jersey have to do with anything? A friend who grew up in New Jersey noticed right away that the Midwest had no walls. There are picket fences, strung wire, cyclone mesh, the red staves of snow fence, chicken wire, barbed wire, even electric line. But no walls. My friend defines the Midwest that way—a country woven in wire fence—and he always argues that beyond the lack of boulders in the ground to build walls, the fences reflect something else inherent in the people who live here. You can see through fences, he says. They do not block out the subtle and endless beauty of the prairie and field. But at the same time the fence breaks up that vast and overwhelming horizon into bits of manageable places. The fence builders want it both ways. It is an aesthetic compromise between private property and being part of a neighborhood. A fence allows its builder to say, "I am alone. Separate, not different. I've got nothing to hide, but don't come too close." It is a delicate balance. There are many such balances here between the individual and the community. The fences of the Midwest give us tangible evidence of the web of these relationships.

8. What does the current disappearance of fences and fence rows tell us about the state of affairs now? The disappearance of fence rows could be written off to the use of larger machines with broader turning radii, the lack of animals on farms, the trouble of maintaining the wire. But does it reveal something deeper? The simplest definition of place carries within it the notion of limits, of boundary. Part of what we believe as Americans, indeed what brought many people here in the first place, includes the contradictory idea of a country unbounded, a place of limitless opportunity. In the realm of advertising's easy diction, *you can have it all*. The disappearance of physical fences in the midwestern landscape might represent a transformation, a shift in interior space as well. A rickety, rusty wire fence was the product of the meeting between the irresistible force of individual enterprise and the immovable object of community. Fences snare and enmesh but are flexible, movable, many-gated. Their disappearance could signal to us the release of an unbridled force that is dangerous to community. An article in the *Des Moines Register* on the obsolescence of the township included a picture showing the entire government and voting body of a township in Iowa: a farmer, his wife, and their daughter. The question that arises is this: When does a town stop being a town? What is the critical mass of a community? The presence of fences tells us finally that there are people here, that the land is divided up among them. As people have left the Midwest the fences have come down. Their absence does not bring people closer together but only indicates that there is no one here. Someone will always own the land but someone will not always live here.

9. Where did they go? The roads that have taken people away can also be thought of in the same way as fences—as physical manifestations of our interior feelings about place and the land. As we've seen, they are the quickest way out of town for our writers, our children, our friends, ourselves but also the way back. Roads too form our boundaries. The section roads lie like a net over the land, divide it, define it, parcel it out, and impose the order of place. But the road is also a common way owned by no one and everyone. When we usually think of the literature of the road, say of Kerouac, we think of the road as a conveyor, as something that moves through, something that is part of somewhere else. Yet, it is also part of the things that stay put. We treat the road as Euclideans would have us treat a line—the distance between two points having no width. But the road, the sidewalk, the corners, the squares are rich with metaphoric meanings where once again the individual meets the group of which he or she is a part. The road may bound us, but it also binds us together. The road is a place itself, as a fence row is, and both must be thought of more as transmitting membranes, like skin, at once tough and intimate.

10. *Can you be more specific?* Good writing is always specific. Henry James wrote that good writing is "selected perception and amplification." There is literally a world of difference between using one word over another, "a" instead of "the." As a writer selects words, he or she is making a series of choices that include or exclude parts of the world. William Faulkner called the county in Mississippi he wrote about his "postage stamp of land." Though writers narrow and select, they often cordon off a precinct sacred to them. Readers discover that within those boundaries there are areas of human experience that seem unlimited. Perhaps it is a quirk in the way we are made, but it appears the more specific a writer is, the easier it is for a reader to generalize. In geometry, we know that a finite plane bounded on all sides still contains infinite points. Stories, poems, essays work that way, too. The more tightly bounded, the more restricted a work is, the richer we find it. Author and authority are related words. To be author of a specific place is, in a way, to be its god, its creator. But the place a god creates can never be as detailed as the larger world it is part of, for the writer faces the fact that he or she is limited, mortal. Writing then, by its limitation, by acknowledging its human scale, still participates in something grand. The writer shares in the creation of the universe by creating a postage stamp. In Thornton Wilder's *Our Town*, a character receives a letter addressed to her, her street, her town, her state, her country, her planet, her solar system, and on until it ends with the mind of God. Her thrilled response is that it got *here* anyway. It got here.

11. *Can you tell us a story?* If books are like places, then places are like books. Let me tell you a story. I was helping a farmer during planting. I was driving a tractor vibra-shanking a field of soybean stubble as the farmer followed behind me planting corn. The operation I was asked to do was an easy one, but I don't have much aptitude for machines. I wound up during one pass almost sliding into a ditch of water when I tried to make the turn. Braking, I stalled the engine, and shaken, I couldn't get the thing in gear to start up again. The farmer all this time was steadily catching up. The harder I tried to free myself and prove my competence, the worse things got. The farmer's son was working in the next field. He yelled to me that he was on his way to help. In a few minutes I saw him poling down the ditch on a raft made of old fence posts, and he saved the day. There isn't much to the story. That's not why I told it. What is interesting is that when I visit that farm now sooner or later that little story is told again—how Michael got stuck and Eric came to the rescue. Sometimes it is told to people who haven't heard the story. But more often than not, we tell it to ourselves. It is as if the story is another building constructed a few springs ago. It is a part of the layout of the place, part of the map. This little story takes its place with hundreds of others. The field where I had my adventure is called Cottonwood for the tree that used to be there sixty years ago. When Farmer Brown tells Eric to cultivate Cottonwood, it is a one-word story. The tree no longer exists. The story does. Places exist in two dimensions. They exist in the physical realm, but also in time. I will exist as part of a place on that farm as long as people tell the story. Though the dirt, the ditch, the crops exist; a place needs a person to name it. Cottonwood. It is interesting what we call the documents that transfer land: deeds and titles. The land itself carries its own deeds and titles. To gain a sense of place is to be sensitive to stories about places.

12. Here's your hat; what's your hurry? A sense of place is a complex idea further confounded by our relationship to it. We all labor to resolve two opposing forces in our lives. On one hand we have a desire to be rooted, to belong—literally to be long—in a place. On the other hand, we wish to be free of those connections, to keep moving through. As with all compelling conflicts, this one is not easily resolved, probably not to be resolved. People now move far more than they stay put. By moving we find it easier to ignore those limits imposed on our lives. The fences on either side of the road seem more like a chute channeling us on to some wonderful future. To have a sense of place is to sense limits, to sense our own deaths, a specific plot of ground where we will be buried and where our bodies will become part of the plot of ground. By accepting the limits a place imposes, we gain the ability to leave a mark. By being part of a place, we become it.

Sympathetic Pregnancies

1

I found myself in a room with nine pregnant women. All of the women were in the very late stages of their pregnancies—very late. Their deliveries past due, they waited in this converted surgical recovery room for their labors to commence. All of them were massive. Their shapeless hospital gowns taking on now the sweeping contours of their swelling bellies and breasts amplified their heft by defining it, the fabric stretched taut across the rounded middles. They all were hugely uncomfortable, in pain, of course, and in various postures of steeping agony—standing, sitting, or splayed in a bed. They had all been induced, that is to say the synthetic hormone pitocin had been introduced into their blood streams via an intravenous drip to spark their bodies into productive contractions. And it was working in spades. The spasms now slamming through them were juiced by the chemical, boosted, turbo-charged. The kick they were receiving packed a bigger wallop than if the body had kicked off on the process of its own accord. This was truly gut-wrenching, a doubled definition of "spike" of pain. Some were hooked up to monitors that spit out a graph paper narrative scored with these mountain ranges of ragged edges that finally climbed and climbed—no denouement but only the inked evidence of one endlessly upward sloping excruciation.

I had been told to wait in the recovery room with nine women in the throes of labor by a distracted doctor at the main desk. My wife, on the verge of birthing her first son (birth imminent, the chart had read), stalled in the delivery during the final pushing. She had been whisked off to surgery for a c-section, leaving me alone in the birthing room with the beeping Plexiglas incubator warming up in the corner.

"What are you doing here?" an orderly asked as he wheeled in a bucket and mop to begin cleaning. I told him no one, in the haste to get to the operating room, had told me where to be, where to go. "Man, you can't be here," he said, "I've got to get this room ready for the next one. They're stacked up out there." So I drifted down to the desk and to the distracted doctor who told me to take a seat in the recovery room.

The women in the room began, in their individual expressions of pain, to come into a communal tune. Each whelp or moan began to synchronize, a kind of round harmony. The sound was transmitted around the room, an a cappella fugue of agony. The women peaked one after the other. The last one subsiding into a whimper just as the next reached a muscular grunt and growl. It was as if there was only one big contraction that oscillated around the room or that, in fact, the room itself rippled in one long ululation of a continuous sustained contraction. Nurses and midwives whispered to their laboring patients to "ride" the contraction, and the cacophony in the room had the orchestrated order of the squealing shriek of a train of roller coaster cars. As each woman emerged from her most recent bout with her body (her body that now was not her body but possessed by these biological imperatives and hormonal accelerants that split open a body to expel another body), each opened her eyes to see me sitting by the door. And as they focused on me, as they waited for the next spasm to grip them, I could tell they really, really didn't want me there.

2

In high-school health classes, it once was popular to have the students carry around, for days or weeks at a time, ten-pound bags of flour. The exercise was meant to simulate the weight of a newborn baby and the sustained lugging to condition the sexually active or soon-to-be sexually active teenager to the consequence of sexual activity, pregnancy, and the consequence of the consequence, live birth. The flour bags would be hauled to classes, held while eating lunch, babysat in gym class. Some students even dressed their bags of flour or pretended to change the bag of flour's diaper, an apparent mass hysteria to better imagine this potential semiattached dependent human mass.

Ten pounds! It is interesting that the birth announcement boilerplate contains a space for the newborn's weight. What other formal communication announces that information? Obituaries do not state that, at the time of death, the deceased tipped the scales at a svelte 185. Nor do wedding invitations report the fighting weight of the bride and groom. Perhaps there is just not that much to describe when we describe a baby, a baby so easily disguised as a bag of flour. We are left with the basics. Color of hair and eyes can change, and so such intelligence is rarely shared. The kid's size, the length and weight, is hardly static, and yet it is duly noted along with the name and the time and date of delivery into the world. Most likely we broadcast the heft of the infant because all through gestation it has been the focus, this hidden relentlessly growing thing, this curious expanding loaf, a kind of staple. The newborn remains pretty much that way for months outside the womb, a swaddled package. In short, the baby is an embodiment of human weight itself. It boils down to bulk. Ten pounds!

So after the birth of my sons, I gained a different kind of weight. Where my wife had come equipped with organic cavities to host the burgeoning other, I had to make do with these artificial blisters—the Snuglis, the papoose cradle boards, and canvas backpacks—girded to my body by contraptions of harness tack and strap. I had a baby sling, an ingenious device that looked and was worn like a Confederate soldier's bedroll. I draped it over one shoulder and it rode around the opposite hip, and then across the back. The sling was even made out of sturdy striped ticking and expanded like a kangaroo's pouch to allow the baby to ball up inside the enveloping folds. The tug of gravity then cinched tight, suspending the joey in this simulated womb. I could not resist rubbing this new belly of mine, massaging this living dead weight that only occasionally stretched, compressed beneath the smooth skin of fabric. How my body was contorted. And how I contorted my body simply to bear this childbearing. I discovered the shelves and hooks, the nooks and ledges of my anatomy to shift the baby about, not hot potato so much as a slippery, springy sack of spuds. My hips. My shoulders. My lap. My elbow's crook. Any port in a storm. I piggybacked. I made a swing of my distended arms. The baby rode my butt, my hands behind me, the laced fingers saddling his behind. I was, during the infancy, a declension of containment—hold, held, holding. Even when exhausted I could not shed this limp limpid. On my back. The baby bedded down on my front, bore down, bearing his full and concentrated weight asleep on my belly.

It isn't hard to make the leap. The literal weight that must be borne comes to stand, in a very solid way, for the metaphoric tare a parent incorporates. I was weighed down and weighed down. As a father I grew grosser by the day, by the ounce.

3

During the nine months my wife was pregnant with our first child, I gained twenty-five pounds. After he was born, I didn't lose the weight and actually gained twenty-five more pounds during my wife's pregnancy with our second son five years later. I like to think of it as sympathetic pregnancy, my body so in sync with my wife's that I matched her transformation pound for pound. My empathetic sensibilities did not extend, thank goodness, as they sometimes do, to experiencing a parallel brace of Braxton-Hicks contractions or a bout of morning sickness. It might be that I lacked the imagination to actually rewire my body's endocrine system to that degree of reproductive fidelity. I simply grew.

The weight did settle on my belly. As my wife grew rounder so did I. I suffered only friends and family, even while they admired and approved of the sensual fleshing-out of my wife, aghast at my own transforming body. "Oh that," I said, "the *couvade*," invoking the French for the phenomenon in order to (what?) make the weight gain arty or legitimate or scientific or, at the very least, explainable.

Couvade translates as the "hatching" or "nesting" and was first applied by anthropologists upon discovering cultures where husbands performed ritual renditions of labor in their own dedicated hut while their wives wailed for real in a hut next door.

It helped to bring up sympathetic labor as the reason for what was happening to me, to my body. We like to believe that we have control over our bodies, and for the most part we do. We control our bodily functions, command sleep, order movement. To exercise is to take one's body for a walk. But pregnancy puts a lie to such neat hierarchy of control. In pregnancy the body takes you for ride. You are at the mercy of the chemical equations coursing furiously through the body. The body's biological imperative. The physical results are stunning, sudden, and miraculous. Of course that is to say the "you" to whom the highjacking of pregnancy happens is not every "you." It couldn't *really* happen to me. I could only witness this metamorphosis. And, I guess, while witnessing, I wished to let myself go, to let my body go. Three-fourths of a year when new life is imminent allows the old life to be in abeyance. I let go without knowing I let myself go. I like to think I allowed my body to surprise me with my own generative process. But I believe my body did this on its own. The surprise was real.

To this day I still carry those extra fifty pounds, the current weight of my younger son. I carry the mass equivalent in size to this other person still. I have no other explanation for it. Sympathetic, my own gravidity.

4

The cravings were real but not at all original. Not pickles but ice cream. That fall we drove to Davis Square and Dave's Ice Cream and ordered dishes and cones of scoops and dips after test-tasting the new flavors, working our way through the tubs in the glassed-in frozen cases, collecting the tiny plastic spoons like charms. We drove to Harvard Square that fall, to Herrell's, who was also Dave but when he sold Dave's signed an agreement to stay out of the ice cream business. Dave loopholed his way back into the business on the strength of his family name. We were in a family way and craved ice cream. We craved chocolate ice cream, the subspecies of which (Dutch Chocolate, Belgian, Chocolate Fudge, Brownie, Chip, Double Chocolate, Mousse, White, Dark, Chocolate Chocolate Chip, Chunked, Cookied, Malted, Marbled, Mandarined, Mochaed, Minted, Plain) were as numerous as the other individual varieties found in the rest of the flavor spectrum. That fall we drove to Central Square and ordered ice cream at Toscanini's, asked that the various candies and cookies and fruit and nuts be mixed into our choice, folded together on a refrigerated marble slab. It looked, as the mixing commenced, as if the ice cream was consuming its ingredients, an enriching metabolism. We brought home pints and gallons of ice cream and didn't bother to decant the contents but spooned the confection directly from the container, producing deftly curling glazed and glistening waves of frozen ribbons rolling up into our mouths.

I marveled at the sculptural suggestiveness of this media. I loved how the shop scoops welded together. The balled ice cream towered, mounded, slumped into Willendorf Venuses atop a cone, how that hood ornament of ice cream modeled the rounded belly, breasts, and hips of a pregnant woman. Ice cream could be sculpted into bodies, and ice cream sculpted the bodies that consumed it. It layered and larded the articulated underlying skeleton. That fall, the fall of ice cream, under its influence and in its hands, we became these spherical corpulent snow people, artist's models. That fall our bodies bulged and bubbled. We became these B-shaped beings.

5

The story goes that my father, born at home, was thought to be, until the actual labor and delivery, a tumor. My grandmother, fearing the growth was a growth, ignored the symptom in order to ignore the expected diagnosis, and steered clear of doctors, denial being the only remedy she believed available to her. One hears of things like that happening, variations on a theme. The obese woman whose massive body masks to her and the world this other body swaddled within. And then there are the tumors that are, in fact, tumors but tumors masquerading as bodies. They are themselves the remains of other bodies of cells commencing on a reproductive journey only to lose interest—hair balls, sets of teeth, or even the mummified ghost of a fetal twin absorbed by the other in the womb, pregnant pregnancy, nesting nesting dolls. The belly and the womb may become confused. The swelling of one by all appearances identical to the other. There is the impolite inquiry of the heavy woman as to her due date. A man's beer gut distends in meticulous imitation or vice versa. And there is a further variation of our discomfort in our own skin. Shame, embarrassment, blush—this burning blindness of the body and it costume of skin. You hear of the impromptu birth in the high-school locker room, the bathroom at the prom. The student who abandons her baby after a full term of concealment. No one, when interrogated in retrospect, suspected, the complete camouflage of the body by the body. No one was able to distinguish the metamorphic growth spurts of an adolescent from those spawned by the spawn within. The body is so much about the Body. It grows, and it grows.

6

I do not faint at the sight of blood. I do faint at the mention of the word "blood." It has to do with the vagus, that vagabond cranial nerve that wonders down the neck and thorax and on into the belly. It is the conduit for sensation in a part of the inner ear, the tongue, the larynx, and pharynx, and it motors the vocal chords while it stimulates secretions to the gut and thoracic viscera. My friend, a doctor, called it "one very interesting piece of linguini." An overactive noodle can send the pulse racing and the blood pressure crashing, the electric schematic of sympathetic suggestion. In an instant the blood rushes to my feet, my wiring for some reason shorting out with this outsized response. I'm sensitive. To what? To words. I weathered the witnessing of the births of my two sons attending the attendant fluids, flesh, and surgery. But merely typing the above, thoracic viscera, had me going. I think it is the Latinates, the antique Greek, that medicine employs to sound disinterested that tweaks my vagal response. Doctors have this desire to explain, to render in that dispassionate vocabulary the description of the body. It backfires with me. Laceration for cut. Contusion for bruise. Hemorrhage. I'm more comfortable with bleeding. The impasse that necessitated my first son's birth by cesarean section was described as cephalo-pelvic disproportion. My heart, *kardia*, skips a beat, arrhythmic. These words for me are engorged, obese with what? Meaning? No, more than meaning. They are viral. They get under my skin, into my system. The codes wired into language still thrill my own harmonic neural strings.

I will tell you a secret. In college I wrote my stories and poems in the medical library, and between insights or inspiration, I sacked the stacks, looking for anatomies and dissection manuals, diagnostics and the casebook descriptions of diseases to read. They would produce in me when I read them a kind of high. These simple combinations of letters, of words, of sentences sparked a collapse of my involuntary systems and, in fact, revealed the existence of those invisible involuntary systems by this very intimate disabling. Mere words could do that. Make me sweat, pale, lose consciousness, collapse. The words about the body took on body. Words were impregnated with meaning, with power. Words have mass, weight, density, gravity. Words have a physics all their own—bodies in motion, bodies at rest.

7

She could keep nothing down. The paradox of morning sickness. Without ingesting any food she grew larger. The logic of dieting was busted. She busted open. The body reworked the material on hand, stored in a snub to entropy, a conservation of matter and energy. This was spontaneous generation. She was sick to death and brimming with health.

There was the time during her pregnancy where she could only stomach white food, beige food at best. Yogurt, rice, mashed potatoes, and oatmeal. As I remember this now, it seems I spent forever making oatmeal in the mornings so that she could get out of bed. I became attuned to the amount of water I added, the amount of time it took to boil. The consistency of the final gruel seemed vital. Too runny or too stiff would trigger another round of debilitating nausea. I was Goldilocks daily searching for this mean, obsessed with food that finally in the fairy tale seemed disconnected from nutrition, diet, weight gained or lost. I remember trying to secret a few raisins, disguised as lumpy clots of cereal, dusting them with camouflaging nutmeg or cinnamon that only initiated in her a gag reflex and revulsion. I finished up the starchy intolerable repasts, thinking I shouldn't let this go to waste, standing before the sink, the stove with a bowl and spoon, eating whitely.

8

There is so much we don't know about pregnancy. For instance, the reasons my wife lost two before the first baby was born and then lost two more before the second. At the time all the doctors vaguely indicated not to worry until the third miscarriage in a row, citing the hopeful notion of diagnostic drift to explain their nonchalance. They figured that miscarriages had been happening with similar frequency and number for all of human history; it's just that now our diagnostic tools were better able to record it. No worry. Come back if it happens again, we were told. The drift of such drift, however, becomes its own explanation. Miscarriages go unexamined—no longitudinal studies, no clinical analyses. Mothers who want to pursue the causes, of course, lose interest when the next pregnancy takes and goes to term, any study of past outcomes forgotten in the time-consumed present moment. We forget to remember. So no one knows. It's a mystery.

All her life my wife has dreamed this rather common dream. She is falling. As she falls she thinks that she is falling and that she is going to die. She plummets, closes on the ground. And then wakes up. Sleeping after she delivered her first baby, she had the dream. She was falling. But this time, as she fell, she didn't think while she was falling that she was going to die. As she fell in her dream, she thought: "Who is going to take care of my baby?" Poets are drawn to a word like "cleave," a word that contains a meaning and simultaneously its opposite meaning. My wife is a poet. Birth is a cleaving and a cleaving.

After the third miscarriage my wife asked the young athletic attending physician when she could start up again. The doctor, perhaps distracted by her charting, perhaps simply self-absorbed, answered that my wife could resume exercise in a few days, later today if the signs indicated. Had we interrupted, with our emergency, this doctor's daily jog, her own regimen of working out? She was wearing running shoes, her hair tied back, sweats. Was she assessing my wife's bulked up body differently now that the body was no longer bulk for a purpose, was no longer pregnant? Time to get back into shape. Into shape. As the saying goes you can't be half pregnant. My wife in an instant had become out of shape. The doctor had misunderstood. My wife was asking how long before we could start again to have sex, to make a baby, to be pregnant. She wanted to get back into that shape.

9

We took pictures. A few days before she was due, she took off her clothes and posed in our sunny living room. There is an extremity to the nakedness during labor. The clothing of modesty is readily shed. The staged renditions of the moment on television and in movies are hilarious with their persnickety management of drapery and screens. We are all born naked. My wife had back labor, and for a while a warm compress on her lower spine helped relieve the pain. Until it didn't. She had dilated, was in the part of labor called transition. She had changed. I applied the heated towel again. "What are you doing?" she screamed.

"It feels like you are ripping off my skin!" This nakedness was beyond skin-deep.

Back to the pictures, to the evidence of that body. We marvel still at its transformation. There is the apparent impossibility of it. How could it possibly work? It is freakish in proportion and scale, gravity-defying and grave. There is a luxuriousness as well. The skin, yes, glows. The darker skin of the aureoles, the eyelids, the lips grow darker. On the center line of the belly a vertical line appears running from the sternum, circumventing the belly from pole to pole. The telltale sign of the stomach's rectus muscle's separation, split open like, well, ripe fruit. You can't help it—all the clichés are true. The pregnant body is not a human body any more but a metaphor for ripe, for full. My wife no longer recognizes herself in the pictures. It was a strange visitation, her body inhabited both by a new body and this other body built to birth the baby. We look at the pictures with nostalgia and anticipation. Birth imminent. For me the pregnant body is freakish but irresistible. It is as if the human species is made up of three genders, this new other one, this thing. Or more exactly that the two sexes give birth to this new species. This other other. Obstetric, that Latinate word, means to stand in opposition to. I am sympathetic. But, finally, I have no choice. I must, we all must, wait on it.

Seven Dwarf Essays

1

Growing up, my son always said that when he grew up he wanted to be a seven dwarf. That was how he said it. "I want to be a seven dwarf." It was funny, of course, because he wanted the most out of that expressed desire. He wished to be both a dwarf—an interesting aspiration in itself—and all seven of the Disney alternatives at once. And this use of a singular plural could have also meant he also meant he wanted to be a whole new category of dwarf, an eighth dwarf—beyond Sleepy, Grumpy, Sneezy, etc.—while still retaining the magic completeness of the whole tribe, the one and the seven. Part of the gang but separate too. He wanted to be both uncharacteristic and characteristic at the same time. He was learning to sort by sorting. This bent had shown up quite early. In the crib he watched the floating flotilla of four stuffed bears circling above him, suspended from the twirling arms of a wind-up mobile. The bears were identical save for the different colors of their matching overalls. I cut them down when my son was sitting up, and as soon as he could, he sat for hours, it seemed, and arranged the bears in a line—red, blue, green, yellow; green, red, blue, yellow; blue, yellow, red, green. It seemed to be in his blood, this four-letter alphabet like the code in DNA. Later it would be flags—he could recognize all the different state flags—then di-

114

nosaurs, Power Rangers, Pokemon. Even now, in the next room while I type this, the teenage version of my son has been at it for hours, arranging the song titles, the artists, the lyrics on the expanding electronic litanies of his iPod. But nothing has ever quite taken him like the Seven Dwarfs did. Not the bears or the flags or the toys or the cards or the songs. "A seven dwarf," he answered when I asked.

2

When I was growing up my favorite comic book was *Adventure Comics*, featuring the Legion of Superheroes, kids roughly my age endowed with various powers—strength, speed, smarts. One hero could inflate and bounce. One could grow small. One could grow tall. One turned invisible. One turned into anything at all—chairs, rocks, light poles. The girl who could split into two, once could split into three. But one self had been killed long before I started reading the series. The twins treated their missing sister like a phantom limb. What I liked best was knowing that each hero had a specific weakness. Ultra Boy had ultra powers of strength, speed, etc., but could only use them one at a time. Then there were the cousins from ill-fated Krypton, Superboy and Mon-el. One could be mortally injured by Kryptonite that could be shielded only by lead; the other was vulnerable only to lead. The weaknesses and strengths were interlocking and always exploited by this month's villain. It was never the whole legion who did battle, only some subset, a team of seven, say, a lineup always shifting. Though they were heroes, those kids were freaks, of course, accurate metaphors for their teenage readers' sense of strangeness. They came by their powers by accident—swept by cosmic dust, blasted by gamma rays. Or did they simply drink the wrong drink? Issue from the star-crossed combination of parents? And there is that fatalism in their genes, the chromosomes those modern threads spun, stretched, and snipped by the three sisters. We all embody our own ancient tragedy—the very stuff that allows us to thrive as a race might well be the fatal flaw, the circumstance of our own demise. The fourhanded carbons are the little gods that destroy and create. The oxygen-hungry human brain we are so proud of is an accident, and the pride the brain can conjure will be the very thing to cause our extinction. It's an old message, these fatal flaws. I remember teenage superheroes sitting around their clubhouse (they had a clubhouse!) lamenting their fates, wishing they could be like other normal teenagers of the twenty-fifth century. Or I think I remember them wishing for that. But other "normal" teenagers are never normal. Or the normalness of teenagers never feels normal. The Legion of Superheroes characters embodied the body growing up, an analog of that awkwardness. It was the theater of between-ness.

3

"Line up!" my son commanded me, his mother, his grandparents, his babysitter. We added up to seven, and we lined up. "March!" he would then command, and we marched. The previously distributed simulations of shovels and picks were at slope arms over our shoulders. A few of the implements were actual scale models of picks and shovels but some were toy golf clubs, an umbrella, a plain old stick. Outfitted, we marched. "Sing!" We sang "Heigh Ho!" as we marched. It was this part of the movie my son returned to over and over, this going off to work. He learned very early to manipulate the remote for the VCR. He marched the Seven Dwarfs over to the mines and back, studying the formation. Disney aided the obsession by producing a videotape of excerpted songs from a variety of films in its vaults. The Dwarfs marching and singing while they did so was one bit featured. We made it to the couch. "Dig!" and we dug, mining the cushions and pillows. We sang: "We dig, dig, dig, dig, dig, dig, dig, in a mine the whole day through!" And took a breath and sang: "To dig, dig, dig, dig, dig, dig, dig, that's what we like to do." I never understood the accepted conventional wisdom about attention span and the modern child. We marched endlessly. We sang for hours. We dug to China and back. It was I who always lost interest, attention waning. I called the marches to a halt, rained on the parade. The other adults becoming self-conscious again, put down their tools, brushing the dust from their clothes. I distracted my son (who was redistributing the tools, reordering the cadre of dwarfs before him as they struggled up from their knees) by flipping on the TV, the accepted accused culprit of expanding the attention deficit, the supposed modern distraction. He scanned the tape and found the marching, the digging, and sent the images of the dwarfs back and forth on the screen. He watched as if it were the replay of the scene he had just finished staging, an actual record not simply another version. He worked the buttons of the remote, pored over the images. Maria Montessori said that a child's play was his work, or was it a child's work is his play? In my stupor I thought it doesn't matter. It works both ways.

4

I remember the exact moment my son transformed. It was at a school carnival, an annual event, we had attended since he was in second grade. Now he was in sixth, and although the booths and games of the fair remained constant, he was changing, literally growing, lengthening, stretched out. We drifted together over to the dunking booth. A friend of his, already wet, was on the bench, taunting the hurlers as they wound up. We watched the action side by side. Without thinking, I draped my arm around his shoulders. Instantly, I felt him tense at the touch, and immediately he began to wilt and melt away, twist out from underneath my half-embrace. It was almost botanical, leaves curling up in contact to some toxin.

In the movie Snow White mistakes the scaled-down house and furnishings she stumbles on in the forest as the habitat of children. She herself is, as they say, but a child, a child lost in the woods. Or until very recently Snow White was indeed a child. She now finds herself in the woods because one day, without her knowing it, she crossed some line from child to adult. That day the Magic Mirror's magic radar noticed that she was no longer what she had been. She became "the fairest," a code for pubescent, I suppose. Now she could be "seen." The mirror reflected that fact back to the Queen, her evil stepmother. I always ask why that day, why this one particular day? Did Snow White generate the final cell of her milky skin that morning, grow the final significant eyelash? Pubescence also suggests sprouting down or fine hair. Did the last of the downy coat sprout? Or shed? Did her lips happen to blush the proper shade of red, her eyes refract, at last, the right frequency of sparkle? Something made her euphemistically "fairest," this final part of the puzzle. One day. It was a Thursday, I guess, and the world changed. In the forest, breaking into the Dwarfs' house, she mistakes it as the house of lost children. She identifies with their lostness. She is lost. And maybe she sympathizes with their childness. She herself was recently a child. She suspects, however, that something has changed. She is no longer a child. She doesn't fit into any of the beds she finds, uses all the beds in the house for her bed. And later, when the Dwarfs return from mining, they peek over the beds' footboards, seven Kilroys Were Here. She awakes, startled to discover that the children she anticipates are not children after all. "Why," she says, "you're little men!"

Now I think of another moment, another scene from when my son was much younger. One day, I was driving in the car. My son was strapped into his car seat in the back. As I adjusted the mirror it reflected him, stuffed into what seemed to be an undersized bucket. I was taken with how he had changed, grown larger, and I considered for a second the disclaimer printed on the outside mirrors of such reflected distortion: Objects in mirror are closer than they appear. But I couldn't help asking him, "When did you grow up?" Without hesitating he answered, "Night time."

5

Living in Oblivion is a movie about making a movie. There is a dwarf in one scene of the movie being made in the movie. It is a dream sequence, and the dwarf hired to play a dwarf in the dream is directed to laugh. The actor asks the director for his motivation. And the director shrugs, offering only that it is a dream. After several unsuccessful takes the dwarf finally erupts, condemning the use of dwarfs in movies, in stories. Dwarfs, he says, are always in cinematic dreams. The only work he can get as a dwarf actor is in playing a dwarf in a dream. "When you dream," he asks the director, "do your dreams have a dwarf?" The dwarf actor eyes the director, who is considering the question. "I'm a dwarf," the dwarf says, "and I don't even dream of dwarfs."

I wonder sometimes why Disney World and all the worlds of Disney are such hits. Why do certain things take us? Why do certain aesthetic arrangements succeed? Why, of all the flavors in the world, should a cola catch on? Why that cartoon mouse or that cartoon dog? The images created by Disney crowd out any alternative Alices or Snow Whites or even Dwarfs. Sometimes I think it is genetic, that people are predisposed, attracted naturally to certain combinations of things, hard-wired to respond instinctually as they do to an infant, say, or a puppy. I read somewhere of Mickey's graphic evolution, his transformation from the ratlike steamboat Mickey to the high-foreheaded, big-eyed, shorter-nosed, babylike Mickey we all know. And love. Disney World is the place dying children wish for. As a last wish! Stanley Elkin's novel *The Magic Kingdom* even features this curiosity. A tour of seven terminal children (their maladies roughly analogous to the Disney dwarfs' characteristic monikers—the "Sneezy" is a child with cystic fibrosis, the "Sleepy" child has narcolepsy, etc.) is trucked off to the Florida theme park. The children in the novel try to make it clear that this manufactured happiness of this happiest place on earth is not making them happy. It isn't their last wish at all. They long for a chance to grow up, of course, and seek in the sexless magic kingdom a chance for sex. An ultimate ride, their first and last roll in the hay. They desire to desire. They wish their illicit wish.

Disney World is a deathless place, simply enough. And I think of all the dying children who will never grow up, sentenced not only to an early death but also to an adult's version of an early death. Better to die than to grow up. There is, in the real Magic Kingdom, this studied confusion between life and death—the robots and androids, the elaborate costumed characters, the endless parades, the "cast members" sweeping, sweeping and smiling, smiling. The Main Streets ageless, frozen in time just in time.

Perhaps it was just the names. Disney was the first to name the dwarfs in the old story. No, I take that back. According to Richard Holliss and Brian Sibley in their book *Walt Disney's Snow White and the Seven Dwarfs and the Making of the Classic Film*, an English artist, John Hassall, did name them in an illustrated edition of the story in 1921. He went with domestic utensils and pantry products—Plate, Spoon, Knife, Fork, Wine, Bread, and Stool. Holliss and Sibley include the brainstorming list of names from Disney's preproduction. Scrappy, Doleful, Crabby, Wistful, Daffy, Hoppy, Soulful, Awful, Graceful, Flabby, Goopy, Puffy, Hotsy, Shifty, fifty names in all. On the list are five of the final seven. Dopey and Doc were afterthoughts, it seems. A doctor friend of mine told me she always liked Doc, of course, not just out of professional courtesy but because he is the only noun name among a legion of adjectives. The adjectives grow into nouns once they are used as names, characteristic becoming character. My son could do a pretty fair impression of Grumpy. I would egg him on. "Be Grumpy," I would say, and he would cross his arms over his chest and lower his brow and frown, pouting, tilting his head down to look at you through silted eyelids. This was his face when he was truly grumpy, when he would register his frustration perhaps at having the dwarfs' march choreography go wrong. I was taken by the performance. I recognized myself in his clouded visage. After working for hours on a rustic portrait of the dwarfs he would howl and destroy his work. Not right! Not perfect and turn back to the same task. How silly, I thought, unable to see what he saw, unable to see the flaw in what he saw. Until I saw myself in the scaled down drama before me, my own unselfconscious grumpiness, my idiosyncratic grumbling over a spoiled draft of an essay or story I was working on, an adult version of this play. These names, these dwarf names, are like labeled portals, doorways into adult attributes. They are gateways between these separate worlds of child and adulthood. Bashful, to me, seems the most adult, a late stage of maturation, the growing awareness of self. I am thinking of those experiments with children, their foreheads smudged with ashes without their knowing, released into a room with mirrors. Only those at a certain age will the notice the smudge on the forehead in the mirror and then try rub it off. The rest are oblivious.

6

Growing up, my son continued to stage dramas. He acted in his high-school plays. I watched him in Neil Simon's *The Good Doctor*, a play made up of seven plays based on the stories of Anton Chekhov. There is in *The Good Doctor* a continuity character named "Anton Chekhov" who often narrates, in a stage manager way, the various vignettes. In the final play within a play, my son played the young Anton Chekhov, and the Anton Chekhov character took on the role of Anton Chekhov's father. The action presents the moment Anton Chekhov's father takes his son, Anton Chekhov, to a brothel on his birthday to make him a man. I sat in the high-school theater surprised, a little taken aback at the maturity of the theme. My son was a freshman. I hadn't known what would transpire on stage. I had asked him if he would like me to run lines with him while he was in rehearsal, and he had always refused. So now I watched my son take part in a depiction of a father facilitating his young son's initiation into manhood. And this construction of the drama contained within it this strangeness, this reversal of roles—the son in retrospect imagining the father at the moment the son was to become a man. I watched from the darkness. My son was very good, I thought, playing a son on the cusp of growing up. He had been in other plays. I see now he had been in plays all his life. He had started by auditioning for parts in the local children's theater. He played the mysterious old man in *James and the Giant Peach* who brings the magic seeds to James. But here he was playing a son hesitating on a threshold, a gateway concocted by his old man, who was having his own second thoughts about this initiation. But in the end, the play I watched actually enacts its opposite. It takes a turn. It is a false coming-of-age story. The epiphany is that there is no epiphany. The moment of epiphany has come and gone. Instead, the "father" and the "son" realize that now is not the time, that there still is time. Before they even enter it, they turn away from the brothel; they turn back home. Dramatically this turn is done with a name. Turning away from the brothel, the father calls his son back from the brink with the affectionate diminutive. "Antasha," he says, smoothing the boy's hair. My son's real name is Anthony, named for my father, though he has always gone by his middle nickname Sam. After the show I greeted him in the bright sunlight—it had been a matinee—praising his performance, his work. I was surprised by the story. I had been fooled completely, I told him. I believed everything. Outside the theater, in the sunlight, I wanted to go back in time. I wanted time to stand still. "Antasha," I said to him in his full makeup and costume, "Antasha, that was perfect."

7

I grew up in Fort Wayne, Indiana. When I was a child my father took me to see the dwarf houses on the north side of town. There was a little village of dwarf houses, six or seven of them, tucked within a neighborhood of larger houses not far from where the river curved toward the hill where Johnny Appleseed is buried. The dwarf houses looked like the regular houses around them except for their size. The houses were smaller in every regard. The scale was dwarf scale. They were bigger than play houses. They were smaller than house houses. Their parts and the materials used in the construction—the doors and windows, porches and chimneys, the shingles and clapboards—were identical to my house save that they were a quarter of the size. We drove back and forth on the road in front of the houses. The mailboxes on the street were the regulation-sized mailboxes but the pole they were perched on was thigh high. My father pointed out how big the meter boxes looked, how the parked cars in the driveway were like regular parked cars, how the silver propane tanks, well, dwarfed the houses like zeppelins moored to their hangers. I suppose we were waiting to see who would emerge from the tiny doorways to check the mail or pick up the paper or water the postage-stamp-sized lawn. We never did catch sight of any of the inhabitants. My father had heard that this was a winter camp of traveling performers. The houses were empty most of the year, the owners on the road with carnivals and sideshows. But even that we were never able to really prove—probably an urban legend. I took my son to see the dwarf houses. He was then the age I had been when my father first took me to see them. It was Christmas and there were little icicle lights hanging from the miniature eaves, halfway down the side of the houses. You know the feeling when you return to look at the houses you grew up in or when you haunt the neighborhoods of your childhood? You have the sensation that everything is smaller—the houses, the trees, the lawns. Memory gives you a map more detailed than the original. The original is underwhelming, shrunken, contracted, lacking. But visiting the dwarf houses I had visited again turned out different. The dwarf houses seemed larger than I remembered them. I drove with my son back and forth around the little grid of narrow streets lined with the dwarf houses. There were lights on, and the Christmas decorations twinkled. The walks had been shoveled and the snow piled up into piles. Smoke seeped from the chimneys. We didn't see anyone. So I drove over to my old neighborhood to show my son the tiny tiny house where I remember growing up.

Sixteen Postcards from Terra Incognita

Numbered in the way they were written,
not the way they were delivered

One of Sixteen: Wish You Were Here

The poignancy of postcards stems from that expressed or, at least, implied desire: Wish you were here! Penned when "here" is so *not* "there" yet addressed to a "you" important enough to make the "you" who writes the postcard forgetful of the "here" where that "you" writes. To write a postcard is actually (in the midst of not being there but being here) to transport yourself to the "there" of the addressee. The genre of the postcard embeds an address in its text like the ghazal insists upon the encoding of the poet's name into the verse. To write a postcard is to caption its caption, to continually locate and place yourself in a place all the time imagining another place, the "there," of the recipient.

Two of Sixteen: Thinking of You

The postcard is place inscribed, dramatized, and animated. It is a place that moves. A piece of place that has broken off and . . . I like to break the proscribed boxed boundary of the space "This Space for Message" message. I write on the photo, verso.

I arrow in on the window, the third floor, third from the left. I affix the legend: I am here. There are other windows on the card. Think: the stamp is the postcard's postcard. Thinking of you! Indeed. Thinking of you, there, thinking of me, here, wishing you were here with me, me there with you. The postcard is a koan of place, our having to be somewhere, and our relationship to place and to each other. It is a place, a place in and of itself. Thinking of you! Wish you were here!

Five of Sixteen: Why *Fort* Wayne

It is hard to imagine now but for a while this plot of ground was to die for. Three American forts were built here. Four French. Three British. The Miami and the Shawnee each had fortified villages. There were massacres, ambushes, running battles, forced marches, insurgences, sieges, conflagrations, surrenders. Torture. Spy Run Creek, it is said, ran red with blood. This place was, for a while, geopolitically present. And place always contains its component of time. A strip of ten miles of land, a continental divide actually, that separates the Great Lakes Basin from the Mississippi Valley, was strategic if one moved around by water. But we, long ago, no longer moved around by water. And this contested portage, overnight, became, quite literally, just another backwater, no longer bothered to defend. Attention shifts and drifts through time. It lights on and lights up a place for an instant. Now you see it. Now you don't.

Three of Sixteen: There Is No Here Here

I love the map pieced together from the montage satellite photos (like postcards) representing the United States at night. There are great globs of light, dentritic phosphorescent tendrils netting up metropolises, the pearlescent bacterial glowing culture. And then there is the negative space, the absence of light, the empty negated vastness. I imagine that in the black blankness the grid of place is waiting to be sparked, that it is a story or a poem that provides the juice, switch it on. How does a place become a place? Donald Barthelme in "The End of the Mechanical Age" imagines God as a meter reader and tells us that grace is not *like* electricity, it *is* electricity. Let there be light. Write "light" and there is light.

Four of Sixteen: Look Out There

Once flying at night from coast to coast I happened to look out the window and spotted the burning blots spotting, their shimmering splatter radiating on the ground below. There, suddenly, was Fort Wayne, all its distinguishing features in place (the quirky cant of its downtown street grid askew, looking like itself, itself assembling itself before my eyes into a here down there).

Six of Sixteen: The Necropolis Leads the Metropolis

City planners once imagined that cities, civilization itself, sprang from our ancestors' decision to simply settle down. Time was right to build a town. But I like the new theory promoted by the trade that cities were a consequence of something other than a conscious shift away from hunting and gathering, slashing and burning. No, humans changed their practice of burial. They began to bury the dead and tending the graves stopped the migration. Bury the dead and this precipitates the living out of the flow. They hole up. To tend the dead. Tending the dead necessitated construction of shelter, the spur for agriculture, the undertaking of specialized individual tasks. The Necropolis leads the Metropolis, you see, not the other way around. Oh it is the chicken or egg thing, I realize. But I like the notion of tending the dead. Tending the dead, the job description of the writer attuned to the steady erosion, the evaporation of the details of time and place, of everything and everyone's re-placement. Stories can be thought of as vast cemeteries of the past place, affixed now in neat rows of print. How does a place become a place? Perhaps through accumulation of stories. A plot defined by plots.

Seven of Sixteen: The Blue Light Special

Boxing Day, 1965. On the spur of the moment, Earl Bartell, the manager at the Fort Wayne Kmart, taped a flashing blue lantern he got from sporting goods to some scrap two-by-four lumber, creating the first Blue Light Special. The flashing light marked the spot of some holiday paper he was looking to unload. The sale had been advertised. Announcements had been made. But the customers were having difficulty finding the location of the reduced stock. People had become lost in the store. The blue light was a navigating beacon, strobing orientation. The customers navigated the cramped, crowded aisles toward the discounted breast of—if not the new world—then, at least, the next year's promised presents. The place I write about is the place where the Blue Light Special was created. I, like Gatsby, another midwesterner, believe in the ecstatic future. I believe in the blue light. It is both illuminating and illustrative.

Eight of Sixteen: The Indiana Sky

There is this shorthand for place employed in prose. The adjectival sky. "He walked out under the Indiana [the Iowa, the Illinois, the Idaho] sky." An efficient way to indicate a place in a story, setting, naming it. But, really, would we know an Indiana sky if we saw it? Or, if in a story we read "the Indiana sky," what would we see, what would be conjured up in our imagination? That is to say, place can certainly be named, but, in merely naming it, can it be known?

Ten of Sixteen: Sky Writing

Look up. Wait! Start again. Look up "Art Smith, the Bird Boy of Fort Wayne." It is said that he was the first to successfully complete a complete outside loop, the loop to loop. He died in a crash, an airplane crash, in an Indiana cornfield. Art Smith, it is said, was first to write in the sky, the Indiana sky above the Indiana cornfields, marking the severely clear azure blue with a cloudy cursive script. What did it say? That goes unrecorded. And besides, it is too far away to read, and the letters, the words, are already smearing, streaking. The ascender on what appears to be a B is evaporating, the apex of an A is now merely a dull smudge. The sky arrives above our heads—transparent, generic, unremarkable. It is sky. By definition, over everywhere, every-thing. It must be branded, a proprietary geography of invis-ible air.

Nine of Sixteen: The Dumbest City in America

From Fort Wayne my mother calls me in Alabama to tell me that Fort Wayne has been designated by *Men's Health* maga-zine as "The Dumbest City in America." It seems to have been done scientifically, with graphs and categories and surveys. The number of Nobel recipients, library books circulating, SAT scores. "What," she asks "are you going to write about this?" It seems one thing I have written is this, to use the occasion of Fort Wayne's designation as "The Dumbest City in America" as an anecdote in a paper to be delivered at the AWP confer-ence that meditates on the elusiveness of place. I don't know. I don't know. By definition my response can't be very, um, smart. I am influenced by the influence of place, a son of dumb. How does the brain think about itself? "Stupid is as stupid does," Forrest Gump's mother says. In Alabama, when it comes to lists, Alabamans say "Thank God for Mississippi." I want, at this juncture, to pun on dumb, to say something about how Alabama gives voice to the notion of place. That that place has placeness. A silence inhabits whole regions of the world, Fort Wayne, Indiana, for instance. That kind of dumb. In the silence in which some places are steeped, someone will articulate the vacuum. Struck dumb by dumb luck.

Eleven of Sixteen: City of Blue Trucks

Fort Wayne is the world headquarters of North American Van Lines, whose distinctive sky blue rigs wander lonely as clouds continually through the city, waiting for a berth. You see them orbiting on the bypass, idling in the far reaches of parking lots, a herd of them huddled together. Air brakes sneeze; running lights run. They've come to hub, to shift and sort and reload loads, to pool then peel away again, pulmonary pods, heaping beasts. Growing up, I liked thinking of the drifting blue trucks, counted them instead of sheep, each of them, I imagined, tared with another living room or parlor, each trailer transporting a suspended domestic setting, dreaming itself. Animated places crept by, a place parade, a parade of place, places looking for places to go and then going. The whole country, in individual dots and dashes, circulating through my city, the furnishings of its atriums entering the chambered city, this contracting, this expanding heart. And then, in another blue beat or two, beat it out of town.

Twelve of Sixteen: The Happiest City in America

In 1948, *LOOK* magazine designated Fort Wayne as "The Happiest City in America." I ask my mother, who is pictured on the cover with a group of high-school girls huddled laughing at a soda fountain: What is the source of all the happiness? In the water? In the air? Where did it go, she asks her picture, the photos of the photo spread? The photographer had no need to ask anyone to smile.

Fifteen of Sixteen: On the Planet of the Apes

"Where are you from?" Dr. Zaius, the suspicious ape in the movie *Planet of the Apes*, asks Charlton Heston, the marooned confused astronaut, who warily responds: "Fort Wayne." And the theater goes bananas where we watched (in Fort Wayne), howling, raucous primate applause. I believe we all wanted the film to stop and start over again and return to the place again where a made-up character uttered his made-up hometown that happened to coincide with our real hometown. I have heard people on vacation visit fictional places, send postcards from such places. Greetings from Green Gables, say, Sunnybrook Farm, say, Field of Dreams. Places that have become (through fiction) real. This real place (Fort Wayne) is authenticated by a bit of fiction, a bit of fiction within a fiction.

"Where are *you* from?" the ape asks.

"Fort Wayne!" Moses answers. The Promised Land.

"Me too!" we all respond, "Me too!"

Thirteen of Sixteen: A Sense of Place

We often speak of a sense of place, that a piece of writing can, at best, approximate a place, suggest the sensation of the surroundings, suggest a sense of sensing. The story simulates, at best, and perhaps needs only to stimulate a vague peripheral nimbus of locale and that is enough to satisfy. A sense of place suggests our alienation from place. It puts us in our place about place. We approach the world on a tack, askance, nuanced, alien and alienated, receding, just out of reach.

Sixteen of Sixteen: A Bottle in a Message

Once I got a coconut from Hawaii. Its hull hulled with stamps. My address and the stamp the only message. From the Smoky Mountains, I sent a little souvenir—a toy black bear crated in a tiny balsa wood box. Often postcards are not about the words alone—not the message in the bottle at all. The bottle itself the message. The medium and the means of transportation, transporting the places temporarily inhabited. Once the postal service would deliver almost anything from anywhere to anywhere if it had enough postage. I always wanted to send a door, unhinged and varnished with stamps, a souvenir of a place I once entered or left. Instead, in hotel rooms now, I strip the door of its framed legal notice encrypted with information that a safe will be provided—that the traveler cannot knowingly defraud the innkeeper—and use it as my souvenir postcard, an accurate indicator of where I'm at, where I've been. This explains everything, I write, an illustration of explanation. I write: Wish you were here.

Fourteen of Sixteen: The City of Conductors

Fort Wayne was division point for all the railroads that once ran through it. The Pennsy, the Wabash, the Big Four, the Nickel Plate, the New York Central, the Monon, and the streets of the downtown were clotted by conductors—passenger train conductors in their dark serge uniforms and freight conductors in stiff bib denim. They moved in time, on schedule with the trains, consulting their railroad pocket watches, carrying their tool bags and flares, ticket punches and key rings. Next door to everyone who was not a conductor, a conductor lived who worked strange hours on long drags to Chicago or Lima or bid highballing varnish to Indianapolis or Cleveland. Next door to us was a conductor, Mr. Kelker, who had lost both hands cleanly cut in an accident. He'd tell us stories. How the city was once a city of conductors, how it felt once to hold time in his hands, and how it felt to live, there, in what was once a destination and how it felt once to feel and how it felt now to feel the phantom feel of fleeting feeling, the subtle texture of absence, the heft of loss, the substantial mass of all that nothing in your hands.

Views of My Glasses

Black plastic frames top the top halves of the lenses that are outlined below with silver wire rims. Silver rivets at each top corner of the frame and at the points where the temples are attached. The delicate clear plastic pads rest on each side of the nose. The pads are connected to filaments of wire that corkscrew with the twist of a dental instrument and then, with a touch of solder, are stapled to the wire frame. A silver metal bridge, etched with streamlining filigree, spans the gap between the plastic brows, grafted into slots, pinned by pins just slightly larger than this period. Men's glasses. The glasses of the Eisenhower administration, the Kennedy administration, the Johnson administration. NASA glasses. Vince Lombardi glasses. Colonel Sanders glasses. Malcolm X glasses.

E

"I will never see you again," the optometrist told me as he fit my glasses to my head. Delicately, with two fingers of each hand at each hinge, he wobbled the frame on my nose and then removed it. He turned away to bury a plastic earpiece in the chemical sand. "These will never break," he said, looking at the sand. "They were built by NASA engineers."

E

A *pair* of glasses. It is like a pair of pants, a pair of pliers—one object composed of two joined similar parts that depend on each other. My left eye has always been stronger, though both have needed correction since I was in fourth grade. My first pair was from Sears. The temple pieces were anodized aluminum and contained, in a compartment near each hinge, hidden tiny springs that tensed the temples to hug my head. They left a mark, an indentation even.

E

The plastic part of mine is black. The company calls it ebony. And the metal trim is silver. There are variations of color. Black Briar. Grey Briar. Mocha. Tortoise. All can be combined with gold wire fittings instead of the silver. All the plastic colors can be molded to simulate wood grain, but that is a whole other line in the catalog.

E

The silver metal bridge piece, the ligature between the contrasting black plastic brows, can look, if you look quickly, like it actually has been broken there and then taped. I have worn glasses taped that way. I used black electrician's tape but the adhesive was gummy. White athletic tape was better. I've taped the temples too, swelling at the hinge, a gall at the fork of a twig. The tape on the bridge turned gray after I punched the slipping frames back up my nose. The frame's internal integral supporting spring was sprung by the break never to be right again. The tape grew spongy and soft.

E

Printed in white on the inside of both temple pieces is SHURON 5¾ USA. The USA is in a generic sans serif type. SHURON, the company name, is more eccentric, complicated, a brand after all. The *S* and the *H* are in caps but the *u*, *r*, and *n* are lowercase, though printed the same size as the *S* and *H*. The *O* can go both ways. The name is definitely a homonym advertising fit. It might also be a pun on a founder's name. Several lines of frames retain "Ron" in their names. The style of my glasses is the "Ronsir." The "Ronwinne," an all wire frame, made its seven millionth sale on September 3, 1946. The brand itself, SHURON, has remained hidden, unlike the contemporary designer eyewear that prints its signature on the temple hinge or temple piece or even on the lens itself.

E

"SHURON" makes me think too of the great lake, a lisp, slur and all. I picture a kind of lake like a lens draped over the bridge of the state's northern peak, wedged on Michigan's cheek. A pool of organically shaped glass, its surface glassy.

E

Others have pointed out Superman's unique take on secret identity. That is he puts on a disguise when he masquerades as one of us, wholly un-super men and women. As a hero he is singularly maskless. His civilian glasses are his mask. The style of Superman's glasses is closer to the SHURON "Freeway" or "Sidewinder," a big, black chassis, plastic all around. In Clark Kent's case, glasses distort the visage if not the vision. I remember that the lenses of his glasses were crafted from the porthole of his childhood spaceship, all the better to surreptitiously deploy his heat vision, his X-ray eyes, without a tell-tale meltdown of the standard terrain material. No one could see how he really sees. Think about it. When Superman uses his X-ray vision all he would see is lead, as the vision would penetrate everything, layer after layer, until the beam ran into the lead layer somewhere that would finally stop it. Glasses do change a face but we read glasses in a certain way. "Weakness," in this instance, is the disguise. The glasses are a visible visual crutch perched on the nose. Helpless without them, stumped and stumbling. Those glasses also clue nearsightedness and manifest in the wearer a concave hunch. Picture books held up to the face; a kid bent over comic books. Superman adopted glasses as his disguise, an emblem of the vulnerability of mere mortals. The glasses show he sees us while he sees through us.

E

Call 800-242-3636 and ask for John Rogers. He is the spokesperson for the SHURON Company. He wears glasses. He will point out that, to a certain extent, the company is now a costumer more than a regular manufacturer of eyewear. A company employee does nothing else all day but handle the liaison work with Hollywood, and Mr. Rogers will reiterate the company line that they are *the* source for "retro" eyeglasses. See SHURON frames, he says, in almost every major motion picture and TV series where "retro" frames are worn. The company could provide a list of such appearances. Their glasses are stars. They are the glasses of stars. Mr. Rogers is less sure who actually wore the frames before the frames settled into a fixed time, were indicative of an era. Kevin Costner, playing Jim Garrison in the film *JFK*, is wearing a pair of SHURON's Ronsir frames. Mr. Rogers is less sure that the real Mr. Garrison wore SHURON Ronsirs. But chances are he did. Style implies change, seasons. SHURON has been making the exact same Ronsir frame since 1947, but the frames they make today are encrusted with cultural quotation marks like the simulated jewelling available on SHURON's NuLady Deluxe line that was introduced recently as a "retro" style. My glasses grew into their self-consciousness. They were glasses, and then they were "glasses."

E

I am not sure that Malcolm X's glasses are a SHURON Ronsir. The design of the device in the upper outer corner of the frame is slightly different. The studs on the temples too are a variation. These fittings are the showy side of the hinge apparatus. They are the decorative rivet heads. The business end of the hinge is hidden behind the frame and attached there and on the temple with two screws, each sunk into the plastic. The screws are set in reverse fashion. One screw is screwed inside out so you can see the slotted head. The other has been screwed from the outside in, its head hidden by the detailing devices mentioned above. In the detailing of my devices, the metal caps are horizontal and inscribed with parallel horizontal lines. The rivet on the frame then flairs out like a spearhead pointed toward the lens and the eye. This detailing, I imagine, is all proprietary, the actual trademarking subtleties of the manufacturer. Look closely at the famous picture of Malcolm X. The one where he is pointing up and outward. He is before a microphone, and his lips are caught forming a fricative, the upper teeth visibly biting the lower lip. Look! The temple piece and the frame piece appear to be capped by a device more diamond shaped, the arrowhead without the shaft, the mathematical symbols (> <), "more than" and "less than" aimed at the eyes. Spike Lee noticed the detail of the detail, or, at least, I think he did. The glasses Denzel Washington wears playing the character of Malcolm X seem an exact match for the ones Malcolm X wears as Malcolm X. I am amazed by this attention to detail. The glasses, and getting them right, are that important. In fact, the rivet heads' > and < are like two halves of the X separated and pointing at each other.

E

It was Jack Rohbach who designed the Ronsir frame in 1947, the first frame to combine the wire rims with the plastic ones. At the nexus of midcentury the frames looked both forward and back. Their styling retained the feel of the recently successfully prosecuted war as well as the sensation of the industrial conversion of war production to civilian consumption. That is to say, the glasses' design seemed both serious and delirious. Their style became known as the "Clubman" as other companies—Bausch and Lomb, American Optical—knocked them off. SHURON popped in smoked lenses and called the resulting sunglasses "Escapades." By the mid-1950s half the frames sold in America incorporated the "Clubman" style. SHURON sold the sixteen-millionth pair of Ronsirs on August 6, 1971. Rohbach wasn't a NASA engineer but a vice president at SHURON. They were his glasses but they appealed to engineers. There is a redundancy in the design, a design to their design. They seem to articulate the mantra of the era, the very current hip ethos. Form follows function. Form follows function. These glasses look like glasses. The glasses are all about seeing.

E

When combined in costume with a white button-down short-sleeved shirt and a narrow necktie or bow tie, the glasses in ensemble create a uniform for a type of crazy. I always thought that Edgar Allen Poe's great contribution to dramatic culture was an insanity that seems sane, that stems from rationality in the extreme. Add a flattop haircut to the above accoutrements and you have the recipe for an outfit of that brilliant insanity. It is the look Michael Douglas selects when dressing the part in the movie *Falling Down*. Logic run amok. The glasses, like the other details of the style, try too hard. They are so sane. It is the artifice of control out of control. They are not, not even in their fake wood or tortoise-shell variety, organic. They are the furthest things from organic. They speak robot, automaton, android, machine. A human so attired is aching to fly apart, to fall down, to stop making sense. The glasses are sensible to the point of senselessness. And the resulting explosion breaks up into all angles and lines—the jazzy cubist, vectors of the atomic age. The design of my glasses holds all its various parts of their construction in place, a very public architecture of tension, compression, gravity, and glue. My glasses are edgy, on the edge, sharp and turning sharper. There is the cliché gesture in the movies of the homely woman taking off her glasses, letting down her hair only to be transformed into a beauty. The glasses usually are the homely making part. Girls who wear glasses . . . A man puts on these glasses, my glasses, and he puts on the potential for frenzy, the spectacle of the berserk. The spectacles of the berserk, the eyewear of the berserker. The glasses are way too sane. Crazy, man, crazy.

E

Floyd the Barber on *The Andy Griffith Show* wears my glasses. I don't watch the show, but, occasionally, I will come to rest on it as I flip through the channels. The show has been on the air all my life, and it is on today in reruns on at least four channels to which I have access. The show aired originally during most of the sixties. It was filmed and broadcast in both black and white and color. Floyd the Barber's glasses look best in black and white. Floyd, played by Howard McNear, is constantly startled. The glasses give him an owlish look and, with the white smock he wears, he looks like other goggled practitioners of close work—surgeons, dentists, eye doctors themselves. The lenses distort the eyes, spook them, draw them out. He doesn't blink. The joke is that he never cuts hair but cuts the same hairs over and over. Cut and comb, cut and comb. Then talks to Andy or Barney in the chair. Advancing the plot through talk. His own hair is slicked and shiny, plastic looking, like it's drawn on. The residue of ancient pomade. His hair is an advertisement for hair. His hair, his glasses, his smock, the flatness of the black and white all create the sense that Floyd the Barber has been cut out, a paper doll. The hair, the smock, the glasses have been crimped on, tabs folded tight behind him out of sight.

E

I make love wearing my glasses. I need to see what I am doing when I am making love. So I am completely naked except that I am wearing my glasses. It must be strange to see that. My lover is used to the glasses, perhaps is even clued when in bed I put on my glasses. The glasses and their putting on a kind of foreplay, an erogenous gesture. Still it must be crazy to see me wearing my glasses, naked except for my glasses. I, of course, can't see the glasses I am wearing to see. I see through my glasses. There are moments, when I am making love, when I am imagining I am seeing myself making love, that I am a third party and I am watching and seeing this lovemaking. And watching and seeing this feeds back into the stimulus loop of the fantasy. But the fantasy I am seeing never pictures the glasses I am actually wearing to see. I imagine there are times my lover looking into my eyes is reflected in the lenses of the glasses I am wearing when we make love. My eyes are clouded over by that reflection. My lover's eyes see my lover's lover's eye—a palimpsest, a pentimento. My eyes, my lover's eyes, not really seeing at all.

E

Today in the newspaper on the obituary page is the notice that Samuel C. Sumerlin Jr. has died. A picture accompanies the brief article. Samuel C. Sumerlin Jr. died at seventy-seven though the picture displays a younger man. He is wearing my glasses. The picture is taken in the sunlight out-of-doors. Beneath the lenses he is squinting. The lines of his eyes squinting are solid lines.

The glasses seem timeless here. In part we learn that Samuel C. Sumerlin Jr. was known as "Sam, the Bicycle Man." He lived on Queen City Avenue most of his life. He was a friend to many. I am not sure what the glasses can tell us about him. Did he die with his glasses on? Perhaps in the Heritage Hills Nursing Home the glasses on his bedside table were not these glasses. But those who are preparing to remember him or you who have been already remembering him remember him in these glasses, his glasses. I am tempted to visit the viewing. The paper lists the time and place of the viewing but not if it will be an open casket or not. I know from past participation in the viewings of bodies that glasses are a problem. The dead are meant to appear to be sleeping. But one does not sleep in one's glasses. At the same time the dead must look like themselves, themselves sleeping perhaps. But the fixture of glasses makes most people who wear glasses look like themselves. Often there are the telltale marks left by life-long wearing of glasses to be considered if the glasses are not being worn in the coffin. I have helped undertakers attach glasses to the heads of the dead. It looks finally uncomfortable. I like better the folded glasses, folded and tucked in the clasp of the hands folded on the chest. The illusion of a nap. The glasses, with their ability to fold, to contract, have in their collapsing a kind of off/on switch. The glasses too are sleeping, napping, off.

E

People are forgetting that the man who was Colonel Sanders was an actual human being. Harlan Sanders was born in Indiana and in his lifetime turned himself into the cartoon trademark he has become. The white plantation suit, the black string bow tie, the goatee were essential to the transformation. It was, I think, the high contrast of the look. His glasses, my glasses, do the same thing. The black plastic brow and the white metal rim create a smiling aspect. He smiles, a cherubic smile. His eyes smile cherubically. His frames frame all that smiling, replicate the smile and amplify the smiling eyes and the smiling smile. I saw the living Colonel Sanders once at the Hobby Ranch House

Restaurant in Fort Wayne, Indiana. The Hobby Ranch House was one of the first independent local restaurants where Colonel Sanders franchised his secret recipe. Later he would sell the concept, and the new company would create their own freestanding shops, the Colonel evolving into the revolving trademark on the side of the revolving bucket sign. When I saw the Colonel in the Hobby Ranch House Restaurant he was standing next to a life-sized posterboard placard of Colonel Sanders. They looked identical but for the depth of one. I remember the glasses. How strange they were in the flesh, dark meat and white, but fleshless too, all plastic and wire. His secret was not the herbs and spices but the use of the pressure cooker to fry the chicken quickly. All of this—the marketing plan, the cooking technology—was new but dressed up, camouflaged as very old and traditional. The glasses are the fulcrum of that moment. The smile now is hard, fixed in print. The glasses disappear into the cloudlike creases of the image's smile, explode in a vapor of Benday dots if you look at it closely and for a long time.

E

During my eye exam, I tell my eye doctor I am writing this essay about my glasses. He has never heard of the SHURON Company, tells me that almost all frames now are manufactured in Italy, a few companies in Japan, but most in Italy. There are a handful of firms in America still supplying niche markets, he tells me as he looks at my eyes in various ways. I show him my glasses, and he marvels at their construction and, of course, remembers them, remembers the famous people who wore them. That gets him thinking about new technology, and he mentions laser surgery again as a possible option for me. He attempts to explain how computers map and cut lenses now, making it easy to fit any frames with specific optics. In the past, different frames demanded different specific blank lenses to be cut. "Does this look better or worse?" he asks me through the machine I am looking through. "Read the bottom line." And I do. "Better or worse," he asks again, flipping lenses around in the machine. For a while I wore contact lenses, but the impermeable plastic prevented oxygen getting to my corneas. My eyes compensated, building new networks of capillaries to feed the eye more oxygen. Had this continued, my lenses would be wormy with capillaries all mined out. So I got glasses, my glasses. My eye doctor, who does not sell frames, says he sees the ruins of my now abandoned capillary compensation, ghosts and fossils in my eyes. The damage has stopped. My doctor has a collection of eye charts from around the world. Chinese, Arabic, Korean, Cyrillic. Today I am in the Greek room, the alphabet that looks like a ruin of our Roman one. I think about the big eyes of the big-eyed Greek icons. Their elongated faces and bodies save those eyes from being the eyes of the cute. But they are that big, and they are washed over by the reflected window on the pupil, the glossy stare of Japanese anime. Those eyes are glasses made out of eye. Finished, the doctor gives me a new prescription.

E

In the movie *Enemy of the State* Gene Hackman plays Edward "Brill" Lyle, a deeply paranoid former NSA spook who stumbles into the main plot, featuring Will Smith enmeshed in an elaborate electronic-surveilled chase. At one point the characters repair to Brill's secure hideout. There, in a slow panning shot, the camera rests for a second on a photo of a much younger Gene Hackman, and we are to take it as a much younger picture of a much younger Edward "Brill" Lyle. In the picture the young Hackman/Brill is wearing my glasses. The glasses add depth of time to the picture, of course, and a kind of innocence. The glasses make the character in the picture innocuous, a middle-class father of a certain era, a salary man, a civil servant functionary. The photo in the movie is actually another movie's movie still. The movie is *The Conversation*, in which Gene Hackman plays Harry Caul, a paranoid eavesdropping spook who overhears and misinterprets conversations he is paid to record. The photo that one movie placed into this other movie is, first, an in-joke. And I was thrilled to spot it. But it also creates the reality of this particular illusion created by the films. Both films worry the reality of reality and how sense is made sense of by collecting and interpreting the residue of action or its purposeful construction out of abstraction. Clues are left behind by accident and design to confuse or make clear. I see I see. A caul is a portion of the amnion, the birth sack, that covers the head of the baby at birth. In *The Conversation* Caul covers his head with the covers of a bed so as not to see the consequences of his action. He sees too much. He doesn't see enough. He sees nothing at all. But it's just a movie, an art form based on a trick of the eye, all those still shots racing by fast enough to move. When I watch movies I watch out for characters wearing my glasses. "Nice glasses," I say to the person next to me. I think I wanted my glasses to be my glasses after watching so many movies in which my glasses appeared. I was attracted to those glasses. The frames were empathic conduits. They sparkled and winked. They were caught in space halfway through time. I pictured myself in those glasses, imagined myself transformed by their simple adoption. The picture in the picture, the one where Gene Hackman playing Harry Caul is wearing my glasses (nice glasses!), focuses on the eyes. The glasses are used to focus the eyes, the eye, the Eye, and the I.

E

I return to the optical shop—the one who said he would never see me again after selling me my Ronsirs—to have new lenses made for my frames. My eyes have gotten worse. When I arrive, I discover the office, a small glass box building, is closed. Staring in the many windows, I see the rooms completely empty. I am reflected in the big plate glass windows, my hands cupping my eyes and my glasses in an attempt to knock down the glare. It does not appear the company has moved to a new location. There is no sign left behind directing me to a new address. When I got my glasses here several years ago, the optician showed me several other frames, had me try on many pairs. I was there at the moment the global eyeglass style was shifting once again. In this transition, there were twice as many options as usual. Frame size was shrinking fast with small-shaped lenses. The newer frames were more playful with the way they beveled color into the plastic edges, sandwiching layers of color in the frame. But there were still many examples of the previous style with their huge lenses in a simple plane geometry of shapes—circle, oval, square. And there were odd combinations of plastic, the double bridge piece of the massive aviator frames or the migration of the temple pieces to hinge on the bottom corners of the lenses, the temple pieces themselves distorted and twisted. Some looked like bolts of lightning, a series of waves crashing on the ear, or the spiraling meander of smoke. In the end, I had him look up my glasses. He knew exactly what I meant and cut into the huge catalog to the SHURON offerings. "These never change," he said. Except for the "OPTICAL" signage there is nothing left. The building is a shell. It seems to stare back at me. I turn to go back to my car. I can drive with correction. I blink and blink in the bright sun. My eyes have gotten worse. My glasses are like new.

Thirteen Ways of Looking at the Moon Winx

An Essay on the *X*

It is the Moon Winx Lodge. That x does a lot of work. There is the x that visually represents a cartoon wink. The eyes are x'ed out in death or drunkenness, the unconscious x that mimics the XXX labeling the jug of moonshine. At night when the kinetic neon of the sign blinks and winks, what flutters on and off is an X of braided tubes. The man in the moon x's out for a moment, then snaps awake again. And why that knowing wink? The X of the unknown or, more precisely, the X of the not wanting to know, the hidden, the disguised, the censored. x'ed out. It is the X of sex, of course, the ultimate rating. The excesses of sex. Or the string of drunken kisses. XXX. The cheesy lodge is a testimonial for itself: The Notell Motel. X marks this spot. It now is X-rated. *Winx* is a kind of poem. It multiplies its meanings. X times X. It's the cross-hatching of a switch, a toggle. It is the map of the crossroads. One does both in bed. Sleep. Sex. Sleep. Sex. This double cross. These eyes closing in sleep and closing in pleasure. These I's leaning in toward each other, crossed and crossing. X-tasy. X-scape. X-tra marital. "Get it?" the sign says, "Get it?" The sign winxs, and you do, you do get it.

An Essay on Astronomy

One can watch the moon rise above this moon. And people do, parked in the empty Moon Winx Lodge parking lot, arrayed in a drive-in movie semicircle of cars, the pattern shadowing the crescent of the crescent moon floating a few feet above them. People come to just watch this moonlight of the moon sign. This moon lights up at dusk, begins to wink, the stuttering spark, the rippled strobing of the inert gases in the tubes. The road runs east and west here, a transcribed latitude the Moon Winx moon intersects and the real moon traces in its courses. If one's lucky the other moon rises above the pines in the distance and then the buildings next door. The moon rises over the shoulder of, balances on the edge of, the blinking simulacrum of the moon. The sign becomes a kind of instrument—a sextant, an astrolabe, or the simple arc of a protractor and plumb line. One closes one eye and takes aim at the phenomena of this asphalted heaven. One shoots the moon as it moves through the night above Tuscaloosa. The moon is in transit across the moon. The sign's single eye eyes the moon's track, tracking the moon. Its cratered eye peeled and rolling up into its blinking lid. The moons are eye to eye. And the two o's of the "Moon" seem to ogle the rising moon. The real moon turns white like some kind of fluorescent bulb itself. "Oh!" the o says and "Oh!" again the other o echoes. This is glacial fireworks. One "oohs" and "ahs" as the moon inserts itself above the moon. Oh, strange cell division! Then, one can do it all again. Orbit the sign and set up station on its far side. There, watch the moon set below the arching outline of the moon, watch the lozenge of the moon slip behind the moon, swallowed then by the open mouth of the moon, a moon within the moon.

An Essay on the Neighborhood of Neon

The Moon Winx Lodge is in a neighborhood of neon on the east side of Tuscaloosa. The "Flora Signs" sign, exfoliating ever expanding petals of neon filigree, tops the hill above the Moon

Winx. I imagine that company has something to do with this precinct of light twinkling along the street. The Bel Aire Motel's sign, a sapphire waterfall, is within sight of the Moon Winx. A block or two farther west, leading farther into Tuscaloosa, is Leland Center, whose asymmetrical cacophony of neon-encrusted signage disappeared in a recent beautification effort of the Alberta City suburb. The light sparked and flashed but the sign itself, the underlying skeleton, cantilevered and jointed, was framed with contrasting shapes, organic and industrial. Nearby a Mason's lodge in a loft is identified with a second story-hanging pendant of neon, the proprietary compass of the order outlined in pulsing green. A tattoo parlor is tattooed with a blood red statement, "Tattoo," rendered in a corduroy effect of letter within letter, a vibration, tiered in a way that recedes inward or, if you look at it the other way, back outwards. And off in the distance on the other side of the parking lot is the Leland Bowling Lanes, faced with its three-story wobbling pin and planet-sized bowling ball, pockmarked with finger holes and outfitted with rings of neon in concentric circles, a target, that, at night, lights up the illusion of depth and distance as the ball rolls away in ever-shrinking halos until, suddenly, it reappears, massive black and back, the big bang, at the starting point, a warp of time, a crazed loop looping. A new arrival is a Sonic drive-in, one of the chain of identical boxes, the building and awnings clad in endless wirings of light, an architectural "quotation" quoting the past that is still present all around it here. It sits there, self-consciously, I think. It is all neon and all about neon. Neon for neon's sake. Its tubes are not bent to animate or to make a gesture toward the gestures of objects we are meant to desire. Nothing appears or disappears, the old urban hypnosis. Not that. The Sonic is transparently illuminated. Sometimes the tubes of light are just tubes of light.

An Essay on Film

Students set up their cameras in the parking lot of the Moon Winx Lodge. Scenes have been written to be staged beneath the sign. Actors act, play out their domestic dramas with the goofy sign walleyed in the middle distance. Or at night, the sign provides the only available light, exposes the shadows with its backlighting. The sound of its humming neon, a kind of snoring, has been collected on endless spools of magnetic tape or now-bottomless bits of digital memory. The metronome of its switching valences keeps time, ambient meter pulses beneath the ping-pong dialogue of the backlit principles. I like the sign best when it is out of focus, smeared illegible in the background until it is pulled into view, etched in the inky night, a dissolve that resolves the scene, an establishing shot that materializes out of the soft cloud of hovering light. The moviemakers are attracted to the Moon Winx like the moths who can't help themselves. The cameras roll, recording this epic—insect invaders of the moon. It is all so damned atmospheric, this moon. So suggestive. A moody moon. The film crews hose down the empty blacktop, hoping to capture the moon's eel-like reflection in the shimmering pools, the pools already steaming in the hot southern night.

An Essay on Lunatics

She is one of many who walk the streets of Tuscaloosa. They are mainstreamed now from the city's half-dozen asylums. The old railroad tracks curve along the fence line of Bryce Hospital, past the front gate, and then cut through the university next door. A joke often repeated is that a passenger getting off here would be hard pressed to tell the difference between the two state institutions. She follows the old rights of way, her marching cadence matching the verses she shouts. A flock of spondees circles her. She walks each day from one side of the city to the other. As I pass her in the car or as I am walking by, I hear snatches of her ambulatory sermon—a patchwork of damnations, rhetorical questions, ecstatic description, gothic tableaus. Other patients are roped together, mountaineering the arching viaduct, spelunking the underpasses. A city animated by cadres of distracted constitutionals. Old men wander Fifteenth Street, bindle stiffed and muttering, giving directions to themselves and each other while even older men wobble on ancient bicycles, collect crushed cans from the gutters, filling saddle bags made from plastic store sacks. I saw her as I was driving down University. There she was, stopped in her tracks, gesticulating, staring at the smiling moon of the Moon Winx Lodge, silent for once. I watched her in the rear view mirror reversed. The writing on the sign all backwards, her face turned up, trying to think of what to say to that beneficent expression looking down at her.

A Note on Blackbirds as Notes

A blackbird sits on the topmost tip of the crescent moon. Another blackbird perches on the curving point below the bemused cartoon profile of the man in the moon, a bas-relief rookery. A passing horn startles both from their roosts. They become airborne punctuation: a semicolon. For a moment, they form that formation, exponent suspended, the final stroke: a bass clef.

An Essay on Dreams

I like the new evolutionary theory of dreams, of why we dream. An animal more likely to survive is one who can stay still, and sleep keeps one still. Dreams evolved, so the theory goes, to keep the mind busy while the body sleeps. Dreams take the mind's mind off waking, make the mind mind. This sign is a dream itself, a dream of itself—with its flying buttress of articulation, its squareless expressionism askewing every angle, askance glance. In the dark, its various shapes unhinge and float, solid matte slabs behind the wired light, a mobile of rhomboid shadows, polyhedral swatches, interrupted radii. The sign is a dream. The sign is a sign signifying "dream."

An Essay on Attractive Nuisance

There is a ladder leaning against the Moon Winx Lodge sign. It casts its hard-edged repeating shadow on the underlying French curves of the sign's design, striping the moon, a kind of dazzleflage. No one's around. Perhaps this is evidence of routine maintenance. Paint needed to be scraped and touched up. Rust removed with some steel wool. Some glass tubing replaced or reconnected. A bird's nest in a dimpled cranny on the moon's cheek knocked down. The perspective of the ladder is inviting. Sighting up, it seems the side rails slant inward, that somewhere way overhead they will meet, a vanishing point within reach. But the ladder leads only up to the moon. I am reminded of the Italo Calvino fable involving ladders, the moon, and lost love. There are times when the moon seems that close, close enough to climb to, to clamor on. But that is always an illusion, a trick of light, the deficiency of our own limited sensing apparatus. There is delight, though, in possibility. The first rung is beneath your feet.

An Essay on Signs of Signs

I wonder who owns the Moon Winx Lodge sign. Probably the same person who owns the Moon Winx Lodge. The motel itself, brick colonial barracks arrayed on terraces behind the office hut, is worse for wear. A few rooms appear occupied, even lived in, the accommodations now week to week. The place has gone to seed, gone way past seedy. Now, no hourly rates offered for trysts or assignation. No, the house here has the air of flop—buckets with old-style mops and those extruded resin chairs, mismatched, on the shattered cement porches. The owner's let the place go. But the sign out front is another story. It's funny because the instrument for attracting the trade is now the attraction. The crescent moon curls inward, its horns pointing over to the ruined venue. Check it out, the moon urges. It has checked out. But you can't take your eyes off the sign. It looks brand new or, more exactly, brand old, an obvious relic of some pre-interstate motoring past, a past when air conditioning was a selling point, not simply a given. The lights all light. The paint is fresh. From the look of the sign, you would think this is a going concern instead of a place that is long gone. When did this happen? One day the owner awoke from a night of troubled dreams to discover the sign was the principal investment, was worth saving even as the rest of the property decays. Actual kudzu grows up the walls of one of the wings. The pool is fenced and filled in. The sign generates no cash that I can see, and yet it is maintained pristine. Tuscaloosa, Alabama, the South, maybe the whole country is fond of those cast-iron markers. The ones that are erected on historical sites, the ones that preserve memory, the ones that denote some significance. I can't wait for a sign commemorating the Moon Winx Lodge sign to be dedicated next to the Moon Winx Lodge sign. Not in the place where it once stood but right next to it. Perhaps the owner already dreams of this, is not waiting for a committee somewhere to act. The sign has already transubstantiated. It is an existential sign. It is itself. It stands for itself. It is its own memorial.

An Essay on Atmosphere

The novel *Write Your Heart Out: Advice from the Moon Winx Motel* was written by Geoff Schmitt and published in 2000 by Small Mouth Press. It is in the form of a writing how-to manual with insider tips, exercises, and prompts, but the story of its fictional author, down on his luck, bleeds through in a patchwork narrative. The picture of the sign on the cover of the book has been tinkered with. *Lodge* replaced by *Motel*. I suppose the revision was poetic. Motel seems the natural appellation, alliterative with Moon. But in the history of the Moon Winx Lodge, using "lodge" averted ones attention from "motel," its bad rap and rep. For a while the Moon Winx itself was associated with the Quality Courts, a loose cooperative of motels trying to spin the image. This is a classy joint, Quality said. There is something poignant and classic and very noir with the book's whole setup. The writer struggles with his work at a cheap desk in a crummy unkempt room while an oversized neon sign flashes hypnotically just outside the window, the window frame reframing the words, scrabbling the meaning. Geoff Schmitt went to writing school up the road at the university. I imagine him contemplating the sign just as his main character does, absorbing its aesthetic radiation, its atmospheric juice. Me too. That's me looking at the moon. A big chunk of that oversized moon fills my window as well. Its smiling bright-eye stare stares back at me. Then blinks.

An Essay on Night and Day

Glen House Sr. designed the Moon Winx Lodge sign in 1957, added the crowning touch of the crescent moon to the preexisting crossword of the Moon Winx Lodge. He told Rick Stoddart, an architectural writer, that it wasn't so much the medium of neon that excited him but the new Day-Glo paint he had on hand. The Moon Winx sign is really two signs. Night and day. The paint—bright yellow for the moon and pastel green for the placards with the cream-colored lettering—has its own charm. At night, the outlining neon in warm oranges and reds also interacts with the reactive paint. The cooler color tubes spelling out the name, announcing the restaurant (in a different font), the telephones, and the air conditioning, look, in the reflected illumination, as if they have been both burnished and embossed. The sign is scaffold shaped, with Moon Winx running horizontally at the top and Lodge a vertical slash, narrowing where it hits the scalloped base with "Restaurant" and "Air Conditioned" and "Telephones" footnoted there. The moon seems suspended from the craning sign. Its face is a sublime one with pronounced cheeks and chin, nose pugged, arched eyebrows, and a smile positively puckered, a Moon a Lisa. The profile works as the moon's topography, as the ragged shadow cast on a rough surface, a pimpled penumbra. The moon faces away from the road that was the main highway to Birmingham when the sign first went up. The moon then casts a coy eye over its shoulder. A come hither. The moon moons the highway, turning its back on the traffic, both shy and an exhibition. The contrasts are most striking. Day and night. Hot and cold color. The severe angular geometric alphabet wedged next to the sweeping free-hand sine curve of the animated moon.

An Essay on Auditing

The night auditor sits in the office of the Moon Winx Lodge. He can see, out the window, the famous neon sign of the motel, a two-story crescent moon, its man in the moon face outfitted with a winking eye. From where the night auditor sits, he sees the moon head on, the narrow leading edge of the contraption, its wide sides displayed to the cars passing on the street out front. He sees more of a line, a thick slice, the intricate cutouts and struts of the sign all flattened. There is little to do. The vacancy sign in the office window, so understated in comparison, is always lit. The books he keeps have been kept. The figures he adds to the folios have been summed up. Next to the desk is a small electrical box with the switches and breakers for the sign. One switch turns the neon lights off and on. The other controls the circuit that opens and closes the moon's electric eyes. The night auditor amuses himself through the endless night, turning the winking circuit off and on, off and on, off and on. It is a wink inside a wink. When the wink is on, the sign cycles through opening and closing its eye. But the night auditor can make the sign wink just by turning the eye on or off. Sometimes he fixes it so the eye stays closed. Sometimes he leaves the eye open, an insomniac moon. Or so you think as you drive past the Moon Winx Lodge. Who, you ask yourself, is operating this moon? It sometimes sleeps. Other times it is wide awake. And still other times its lids flutters as you drive by, both coming and going. The moon is dreaming. Rapid eye movement. It is a mystery and a gift as you commute.

An Essay on Folly

Call it a folly, a useless edifice where art meets architecture, where structure meets sculpture. The Moon Winx Lodge sign. The architect Frank Gehry's follies always incorporate an image of a flopping fish. The concrete lawn deer, the pink plastic flamingo are ready-made follies. A bowling ball in a garden. Follies are buildings—well not buildings—but built things that are built for no other reason than to say they can be built. They are interesting as things in a context. They are things, and they define the thingness of things. And the places where we find these constructed things gain too. Follies are foci of place. I think of the Moon Winx sign as a folly. It has evolved to a constructed "natural" wonder like a waterfall or more like a geyser. It is an Old Faithful of light and color and on its own clock. I have seen people just stop and look at it, regard it, contemplate it. In Japan today pilgrims are retracing the journey the poet Bashō took centuries ago to the North Country. As he traveled he wrote poems. A cherry tree Bashō commemorated is believed to survive today amid the modern urban landscape, on a pedestrian island in the middle of a busy highway. It does not matter when one looks. The folly expands. The folly defines. A folly is foolishness and it fools you. Move along. There is nothing to see here. There is nothing to read here. There is nothing but this compelling nothing.

On Being

B

"So I have sailed the seas and come . . . to B. . . . a small town fastened to a field in Indiana." So begins "In the Heart of the Heart of the Country," a story by William H. Gass. He began writing it about fifty years ago, while he was living in the town of Brookston, Indiana, about the time I came to be, born in another corner of that state. Years later, I read the story for the first time in a classroom on the third floor of Jordan Hall, on the campus of Butler University, in Indianapolis. I didn't know then that Gass had lived in Brookston. He reveals that much later, in the preface for a paperback reprint of his story collection, where he also admits to B. being an allusion, in his thoughts, to William B. Yeats's poem "Sailing to Byzantium" and to the pun imbedded in B. of "be." And he writes that the town of B., finally, is not anywhere, not any place, really. The story's setting is to be read as an artifice—see "Sailing to Byzantium"—a model, an abstraction at best. This story was not to be confused as biography, auto- or otherwise.

But what did I know? I was a sophomore in Indiana, enamored by the artifice I was reading in the huge limestone ship of Jordan Hall, these words about the place I had inhabited since birth. Gass does say that a former student of his at Purdue University, just up the road from where I sat reading, working as an editor, prompted what became "In the Heart of the Heart of the Country" by asking Gass to write what it was like to live in the Midwest. What it was like. It would be years before I read this. When I read the story, though, I was a literalist, so the first chance I got, I went looking for B.

Bypass

I was on my way to B., entering or leaving Kokomo on US 31, or scalloping around Huntington, Wabash, Peru, Logansport on US 24, or inching along Eighty-sixth Street, Ninety-sixth Street on what was once the outskirts of Indianapolis. I drove on these bypasses that bypass nothing now. It was the landscape of cartoon backgrounds, repeated endlessly as the animated characters amble along, but jazzier, with an asymmetrical syncopation, arrhythmic but still percussive, anticipatory. Gas station, drive-in (hamburger), mall, motel, new car lot, gas station, drive-in (roast beef), mall, bank, new car lot, motel, Wal-Mart, shopping center, drive-in (pizza), drive-in (hamburger), motel, used car lot, gas station, K-mart, mall, drive-in (chicken), motel, mobile homes, drive-in (subs), Target, car lot, mall, gas station, drive-in (hamburger), drive-in (hamburger), drive-in (fish). This was "mature clustering," the marketing strategy whereby a place became a place not specifically but generally. A place to go to, to wander through, around in, in a car, until someone decides to stop. I'll get gas, get food. I'll pull in at that next light, the next block. I imagine a time when all of this will connect, when the real estate along every highway that forgot to limit access (why limit access?) organizes itself into one endless corridor of chance and light and existential buildings designed to announce their purpose, their reason for being. "Ducks" architects call them. The duck-shaped building that sells ducks, the doughnut-shaped building that sells doughnuts. My car slid along, impelled by a kind of magnetic levitation, from one franchise to the next, seamlessly, so that after a while it did seem that the background was moving. I simply sat still, took in this endless pageant of desire to desire. The placeless place. The artifice of eternity.

B

Bainbridge, Bargersville, Bass Lake, Batesville, Battle Ground, Bedford, Beech Grove, Berne, Beverly Shores, Bicknell, Birdseye, Black Hawk, Blanford, Bloomfield, Bloomington, Bluffton, Boggstown, Boonville, Boswell, Bourbon, Brazil, Bremen, Bristol, Brook, Brooklyn, Brookston, Brookville, Brownsburg, Brownstown, Bruceville, Bunker Hill, Burlington, Burlington Beach, Burns Harbor, Butler.

Beta

There is no "bee" sound in Greek. No, that's not right. There is a "bee" sound but the letter *b* does not make it. Think of that—a letter *making* a sound. The word we know as *beta*, the "bee" of the Greek alphabet, the "beta" compounded in the word "alphabet," the fragmented "bet" of the word "alphabet," is pronounced "veta." The "vee" sound. To make the "bee" sound one must use *mu* and *pi*. I have no idea why. What great phonic shift took place over centuries and miles? Sound is the geography of the mouth. The language itself drifts and wanders, sheep clouding a trackless field. The sound shades into the other regions of the mouth, different articulations of tongue, teeth, palate, and lips. The "bah" lulls up against the "whaa" of the *w*. "Basil" is the English parallax of "Vasilli," its slightly out-of-sync double. Our even more English "William" derives from "Vasilli," and from there, its corruption, the strange diminutive, our Bill. Bill. That will bring us back to *b*. Language is all babble in the beginning. Then a sense emerges from the sounds we make. Making sense by making sounds. Bah-ed into life. Balled. Or wailed.

Battlefields

Names of. The South named theirs after the nearest town. The Union stuck with bodies of water. Battle Ground, Indiana, settled on the generic name, taking its name not from the name of the battle (which was named the Battle of Tippecanoe) but from the existential description of the place where the battle occurred. Prophetstown had been the town where the Battle of Tippecanoe took place, at the confluence of the Tippecanoe and Wabash rivers. Prophetstown, an Indian enclave of thousands, was destroyed by William Henry Harrison, later known as Ol' Tippecanoe, after the battle.

The town of Battle Ground grew up after the battle. Its founders seemed not to be able to muster the energy for a more accurate name. Or perhaps the battle itself struck them as so significant. It seemed to them the ultimate battle. It went without saying. It would not need to be distinguished from all the other fields on which other battles had been fought, are fought, will be fought.

For a long time I thought Battle Ground was the B. of "The Heart of the Heart of the Country." Its understatement worked on both a literal and metaphorical plane. Here the internal and intimate struggles of the narrator could be played out in a spot characterized as the address for battles. A town named Battle Ground. Its business was strife, every house a battlefield, every hour a new skirmish, everyone and everything conflicted.

Bypass

My father hadn't listened when his doctor explained what they were going to do to him. I told him as he recovered that it had been a good sign when the surgeon switched his heart back on, that it started up again without a stutter. "Boom," I think I said, "it kicked right on." I had mentioned this as a good thing, as an indication of how strong he was, his heart was, how successful the operation had been.

"They stopped my heart?" my father asked. He couldn't, didn't believe it.

"They can't quilt on the organ with it flopping in your chest."

"How long?" he asked.

"Hours," I told him.

On the other side of the curtain, my father's roommate, who also had had a bypass, was teasing his young doctor. He asked how long before he could have sex again with his wife. The doctor had been sketching out the regimen of recovery, exercises, dosages of pills. He seemed unprepared for the question. The patient's wife giggled. The patient said he couldn't wait to start up again. His wife continued to laugh and snort. My father ignored them. He was concentrating on his own heart, its simple mechanics and none of its poetry.

B-Side

This essay is an accumulation of fragments. It is on the flip side of the hit story "In the Heart of the Heart of the Country," which is itself, by design, a fragmentary accumulation of data. What was left out when Gass selected and amplified his observations? I would love to discover the left-out outtakes, the takes not taken, the rejected jam sessions, the negligible leavings from the other side of the track. In the story, a railroad track guts the town of B., the track that sings. In Brookston, at the time Gass wrote the story, the tracks were owned by The Monon, the Hoosier Line. No map can ever map a place exactly. All maps are distortions. The Monon. I am more interested in the trash left over, the stuff that doesn't fit, like all the junk genetic sequencing discovered in the genome. The thrown away. The empty place that must be filled. The space that holds open a place. The nothing that does not fit. Monon. Monon. Monon.

Battlefields

In elementary school, when I first had to memorize Abraham Lincoln's Gettysburg Address, I confused "hallowed ground" with "hollowed ground." The graves were a kind of hollow, I figured. The ground did appear to be hollowed out of the rest of the world. These precincts are set aside, allowed to lay fallow as a result of armies, often accidentally, fighting each other at these coordinates, crossroads, campsites. If a hidden component of place is always time, preserved battlefields are ways to stop time. But in doing that, they do more. Places that were, for a moment, so briefly populated, so violently inhabited, are now so often empty of people. Especially the battlefields with more obscure histories like Tippecanoe. They seem like the dead zones of seas at the mouths of rivers, where sustaining oxygen has been sucked out of the water. Who remembers? In busy Europe, wars plowed the same fields over and over. The few battlefields that exist in North America suffer under the pressure of the present catching up. The survival of these dead regions seems more likely in the parts of the world that were remote on the occasion of their violent and definitive occupation.

After the battles, the history, the facts of the matter, are done, gone, over. We are left with the residue—the roadside marker, reduced to the inscribed steel plate bolted to a boulder. And this absence of anything. Something happened here, and because it did, nothing can ever happen here again. A sign marks Prophetstown with a paragraph, no longer than this one, of history. A mile down the road, Tippecanoe's obelisk is in a fenced grove of trees, a monument to its own insignificance. The fence allows for a notice that reads Entry Is Prohibited each night forever more after sunset.

Bonneville

I first went looking for B. in my parent's big green Bonneville. I left from Butler soon after reading "In the Heart of the Heart of the Country" in my literature class. The car handled like a boat, wallowed along the secondary roads I followed toward West Lafayette and the archipelago of B-beginning towns within commuting distance of Purdue, where Gass had taught. Battle Ground, Burrows, Buck Creek, Brookston, Bringhurst, Boylestown. After thinking B. was Battle Ground, I settled on Brookston and searched its back streets, navigating by means of prose, on the lookout for landmarks. I never found the row of headless trees, the sidewalk that crumbles into dust. Consulting a ragged phonebook in a phone booth outside the phone company, I found a few names of characters, and, for a second, considered calling the Motts, but stopped myself. The author, I assumed, had consulted the same or similar phonebook during composition, borrowing a real name for the story's reality. Mott, who could top that?

The lights were coming on in the houses as I cruised the streets. It was a pale Indiana winter, with the diminished sun a long way off to the west. In the gloaming, I continued to look for that stand of headless trees until I picked up a tail—a local police car—who trailed me, as curious of me as I was of his town, at a respectful distance until I crossed the city limits on Indiana 43 heading south toward Indianapolis.

Bypass

Jigsaw puzzle pieces look like pieces of a jigsaw puzzle. Each have the telling knobs and corresponding scoops, the bulges and depressions save for the welcome exceptions of the edge and corners. Apart they look almost alike. I like the particular jig that cuts that notch, heart-shaped, a wedge more defined than the simple swelling fingers and peninsulas of other, less radical cuts and curves. My father began to piece together puzzles to pass the time while he recovered from his surgery. His heart had been puzzled back together, and he, of course, in his convalescence pondered the puzzle of the heart.

"You will be sad," his doctor had told him, including among the prescriptions antidepressants, mood enhancers.

The puzzle picture of a bucolic landscape or a placid river that he pieced together made him weep. Exhausted by the effort of manipulating the cardboard chips and processing the sentimental narrative coming together on the table before him, my father had me walk him down the driveway, a journey of a thousand miles, where he fixated on the crackled crazing of cement in a square of sidewalk. It brought tears to his eyes. I gave him a puzzle I ordered from the catalog of the Museum of Modern Art. No picture, just each piece a different primary color and each piece brightly colored on both sides, the heads and tails. It looked easy, but it was harder than it looked.

Butterflies

Indiana rests in the lee of Lake Michigan. As far south as Indianapolis, the clouds produced by this coincidence cast the state in shadow. Gass acknowledges the phenomenon in a section called "Weather":

> In the Midwest, around the lower Lakes, the sky in the winter is heavy and close, and it is a rare day, a day to remark on, when the sky lifts and allows the heart up. I am keeping count, and as I write this page, it is eleven days since I have seen the sun.

In the Gothic gloom of Jordan Hall, whose limestone façade mirrored the veneer of limestone clouds, I read those words and was comforted to imagine that weather mine, particular to me, a map of my own interior state. I stood at a specific intersection of climate and topography. Chemistry too.

Indianapolis had been a sad town then, but years later, when I stopped en route, on my way again to B., the old ramparts, stockyards, and warehouses seemed transformed. Even veiled in its usual shroud of haze, it felt different to be here. I remarked to my host, Susan Neville, "What gives?" Without missing a beat she responded, "Prozac money," referring to the pill, locally formulated, that seeded the weather of the heart while, at the same time, made glad the pocketbooks of the heartland. Naptown awoke in spite of the weather.

It reminded me of another local miracle I witnessed years before, while trudging across the bleak campus. A cloud of Monarch butterflies navigating their migration to Mexico suddenly saturated that grassy strip of mall, oriented north to south, where I slouched toward class. I was, for a moment, completely engulfed, cocooned by their swarming. The raining fall of spring flower blossoms. But they didn't land, continuing instead to swirl and dance, so many I thought the flutter of their wings had reached a mass critical enough to create an entirely new sound only I could hear. A flap perhaps. Magic seems to lodge somewhere else for those who live in the lee of the lower Lakes.

Blue Bridge

When I was home, I borrowed my mother's car, a bright red Volkswagen Beetle, and drove it along the end moraine of the last continental glacier from the most recent Ice Age. I left my father convalescing in Fort Wayne, bent over a thousand-piece puzzle, depicting, when complete, a still life of fruit and flowers. In the borrowed Beetle, my mother had arranged her own bouquet of plastic black-eyed Susans in a vase that was strange standard dashboard equipment. The road, like a river, skirted the floodplain of the Wabash, meandering from the moraine, down into the valley, over the running stream, then out onto the black bottomland and back. I was sailing.

Once, this was the bed of an ancient inland sea, a vast wash-out field from a stalled glacier, a sheet of water spreading out. I tacked; I reached. I thought of stories. Of "In the Heart of the Heart of the Country," of course, my destination, the landscape, which I was again reading and reiterating on my way to Brookston. I thought of a story I wrote years ago, under that other story's influence, about a dairy farmer on this very road heading toward, in mind and body, an absent lover, his absent love. The daisies clouded the dash, obscuring the dials. She loves me. She loves me not. She loves me. Suddenly I came to a truss bridge, freshly painted a cheerful primary blue, the only color in the landscape save for my little red car, its cargo of yellow daisies. The bridge was only wide enough for one car. I waited at its entrance. A traffic light regulated the one-way flow, the one-at-a-time passage. I waited. No car was waiting on the other side. I thought of the valves of the heart, the hydraulics of locks and dams, alternating current, the magnetism of love. I imagined a ghost car approaching, an alternate universe, another journey from another time. My farmer in his Continental. Gass on his way to class, on his way home. Me, returning from another mission through the same pages of these familiar fields. The light turned green and I eased out the clutch, weighed anchor, made way into this parade of other possibilities.

Bernoulli

What did I know of sailing? I am from Indiana, land-locked and a long way from the sea. Yes, there is that pesky easement to Lake Michigan, a seeping valve in its heart, but I grew up a long way from water. I like the ending to the *Odyssey*, where the hero is ordered to walk inland with an oar until the natives he meets no longer recognize it for what it is, mistaking it for a flail. Why are you carrying a flail? That would be me, the land-locked boy, asking. I knew nothing about sailing, nothing about tacking or heeling or coming about. I figured that a sail caught the wind, that the boat got pushed from behind. You could only sail one way, in the direction the wind was blowing. I knew nothing of the principle of lift, of wing. Not until later did I understand that you could sail into the wind, or almost in that direction, in any direction, really, as long as you had a wind. I finally understood the paradox of the wind. When it is most difficult to move, when the wind is in your face, it feels as if you are moving the most, an illusion created in the confusion of your senses. Inching forward, almost standing still, makes for the most interesting sailing; such tacking amplifies the sensation of motion, moving to get into the position to move.

One must read "In the Heart of the Heart of the Country" in a tactful way, sometimes skipping, forward and back, from one square of prose to the next. It isn't so much a series of moments, but a set, a slide show, a contact sheet, a webpage of thumbnails. They can be shuffled, reordered, repeated. I swear when I read the story in different anthologies, sections are missing, and new ones added. Each section floats independent of the others, yet all are borne by the same breeze, the conflicting currents. Paragraphs, like continents, drift apart and together from reading to reading. That can't be right. But it does feel right.

Boston

Once, I found William H. Gass. I was working in Boston, and he was visiting to lecture. I had been recruited to introduce the concluding session of his two-day gig. I was from Indiana, an oddity, and had told everyone in Boston about wandering around that state in search of B., a small town fastened to a corn-field. This admission made me stranger still to my colleagues in Boston, which is the hub of the universe. Quaint to be from such a place, Indiana. It might as well be India. And strangely touching, this quixotic search for an imaginary place. "You simply must introduce our guest," they said and put me on the spot.

Gass was nothing like I had imagined. He had bored the local audience with his current passion, a slide show of amateur snapshots glossed, glazed with his lovely language about the language. Each slide launched an elaborate essay about itself, prompted by a pedestrian picture of, say, an anonymous door-way in some nameless street of an unidentified town in a vague country. I think he was promoting an aesthetic of the ordinary, an anti-aesthetic, but he couldn't help himself. There was a world in each photograph as there are worlds within each word. I have sailed the seas to see.

By the second night, the crowd had contracted to stragglers and hardcore fans. In my introduction, I related the history of my voyages in search of B. I sailed the seas, I said. And I drew their attention to one of the last sections of "In the Heart of the Heart of the Country." Entitled "Church," it recreates a mo-ment of a high-school basketball game in Indiana.

> Then the yelling begins again, and then continues: fathers, moth-ers, neighbors joining in to form a single pulsing ululation—a cry of the whole community—for in the gymnasium each body be-comes the bodies beside it, pressed as they are together, thigh to thigh, and the same shudder runs through all of them, and runs toward the same release. Only the ball moves serenely through this dazzling din. Obedient to law it scarcely speaks but caroms quietly and lives at peace.

I had wanted to make a point, I guess, pointing out the contrast between the things in rest and in motion, the agitation of rest and the quiescence of movement. It's how I feel I felt driving aimlessly and with an aim through the space of Indiana. It is how I felt, I feel, reading the story in which nothing and everything seems, seemed to happen. I sing of what is past, or passing, or to come.

On the way to the reception, Gass told me that my expeditions in search of B. might be beside the point, that the place did not exist. Or existed only in the story, like a variable in an equation. X. B.

"I knew that," I said, "I knew, know that."

Baptism

Robert Indiana, the artist who sculpted LOVE, lives on the island of Vinalhaven, a jigsaw puzzle piece of rock off the coast of Maine. Hidden in that rusting fragment of the alphabet that stands for LOVE is the heart-shaped cutout in the sculpture's heart. It is made by the V-ed rays of the V's angled legs and their curving serifed caps curving inward to form that other, shallower V. What was his real name, Robert Indiana, like Gass, another architect of loose associations between the state of Indiana and the state of love, of longing?

Breast

On the first day of classes I always ask my students where they are from. Force of habit and habitat. "Where you from?" There are always the ones, more than you would guess, who answer that they are from nowhere and everywhere, usually self-described brats of the military, the conglomerate, the academy. Once a woman, anticipating the question, I suppose, or homesick, or both, pointed to a spot on her chest. She was wearing a T-shirt printed with a map of her state. She pressed her finger down indicating the region above her heart. "I'm from right here," she said, turning left and right so that the entire class could see.

Battlefield

My frail father sat, a paltry thing, at the card table sorting the puzzle pieces by color. He had defined the boundary of the puzzle, piecing together the edge. Inside the edge, he added to the mounds of separate hues. Each individual piece was nothing but an abstraction, a cloud of color. He tossed a piece into one pile and another piece onto another. He chewed on what looked like a bit of the sky, considering. He read the terrain, the declivities and defiles. He surveyed the shattered landscape before him, nowhere near the moment when the landscape pictured on the box art becomes the tiled landscape on the table.

Basketball

My father played guard. There is a picture in his yearbook. He is posed in that antique stance, the underhanded free throw. It is a composition of curves. His oval face. The arch of his bowed legs. The parabolic cradle of his arms around the ball. The squashed ovoid of the foul circle inscribed at his feet. The O his mouth is forming. The eggs of his eyes. The twin black scallops of their irises. And on his jersey, double zero.

Baptism

After the Battle of Tippecanoe, William Henry Harrison became Ol' Tippecanoe. The history of a piece of ground is recorded in a deed. Here, the deed was deeded to the man. Of all my addresses, not one has attached itself to me. Nor have I made any place memorable. There are times I want to lose myself in this place or, better yet, confound all that I find while looking. I want to be the fixed point and the vector, the tangent. I want to wrap myself in this field as if it were a robe, rob it of its name, and then roam.

Byzantium

Today Sparta looks so midwestern. Cornfields, fastened all around, surround it. Its streets are arranged in a tidy grid; a green or red tractor putts by. The famous Sparta of antiquity was long ago laid to waste. The present city was built only in the last century along modern functional lines. But up in the hills, in the mountains outside Sparta, above the neat order, I stumbled on what is left of the red brick walls and buildings of a provincial Byzantine outpost, Mystras. The Ottomans sacked it last, in 1453. It isn't touristed much; the crowds more are attracted to the famous marble sites, the classics. Even in ruin it's a backwater, the B. of the Holy Eastern Roman Empire. The afternoon was hot, and I wandered the dusty streets between the intricate piles of rubble, thinking of drowsy emperors.

The few restored churches came equipped with their own featherbedded guards who, honestly, sang for me when they turned away, magnanimously ignoring my prohibited picture taking of their faded frescoes. A convent stood extant in the heart of town, and through the bars of the gate, I watched one old tattered nun sweep the same stone square of the courtyard for the rest of the afternoon.

Bug

I took a break from tending my father, who was tending his heart, to meander around Indiana searching for B. That neck of the woods, pretty much woodless, beckons. Its expanse invites me, its infinite regression of the horizon, its pulled focus pulling me deeper into depth and distance. I get restless after I travel so far to return home. My parents have come to expect it. Tank up a car. I bug out. I never know what I'll find when I don't even know what I am looking for. There isn't much to find.

Here I was going to try to do something with the seventeen-year cicada hatches. Picture myself driving through the hatch as I did one year a few years ago.

Here, I was going to force a connection with their spent shells scaling the tulip poplars and golden rain trees in New Harmony and me tooling through their sawing music, encased in my own carapace.

A friend writes that this last summer the Midwest was plagued with lady beetles blooming when the aphids they feed on bloomed. When the soybeans were cut and the aphid population crashed, the predators moved indoors. "Still in the corners of most rooms in our house," he writes, "you can see them masquerading as innocent specks, trying to hole up here all winter." Innocent specks. In "Order of Insects," Gass's narrator also contemplates the insects that appear in her home, gradually falling in love with the infestation. There is here in Indiana an abundance of almost nothings, no-see-ems, gnats, and midges. An abundance of almost nothing. This is plane geometry. The infinite number of points in a finite space.

Business

"In the Heart of the Heart of the Country" ends with "Business." It is about Christmas in the town of B. The narrator is alone, outside, downtown, listening to barely audible carols being broadcast to set a festive and, it is hoped, profitable mood. I am not sure anymore of how places inform or deflect us.

I sailed to B. again and drifted down the streets, mildly interested by what was happening in each neat house—what recovery, what quiet desperation, what stories were being recounted, what lives lived. But it is more the wrack and spindrift that draws my attention now. It isn't seas so much I ply but their edges. Indiana is an ocean of backwater. It is the vast and empty shingle where everything I can imagine washes up, the beach I comb alone. I got out of the car in Brookston and loitered on the corner downtown where I could picture Gass long ago loitering. Listen: the muffled thuds, the heartbeat of the town. There, the breaking waves of traffic rushing disguised the undertow of silence. My ear was cocked. Blood pulsed through my body. I heard that, too. Cars beat on a tack, heading south, heading north, heading east, heading west. I heard the wind. In the trees. I heard it scour the dust in the gutters, rattle a tin sign. I was. I am. Be. I stood there, as I lost the light, thought of home, and waited for the wind to come about.